Bessie Head

Twayne's World Authors Series

Bernth Lindfors, Editor

University of Texas at Austin

TWAS 882

BESSIE HEAD AT THE WRITERS' WORKSHOP, GABORONE, APRIL 1976.
Stephen Gray

Bessie Head

Craig MacKenzie

Rand Afrikaans University, South Africa

Twayne Publishers
New York

Twayne's World Authors Series No. 882

Bessie Head
Craig MacKenzie

Twayne Publishers
1633 Broadway
New York, NY 10019

Library of Congress Cataloging-in-Publication Data

MacKenzie, Craig, 1960–
    Bessie Head / Craig MacKenzie
       p.   cm. — (Twayne's world authors series ; TWAS 882)
    Includes bibliographical references and index.
    ISBN 0-8057-1629-7 (alk. paper)
    1. Head, Bessie, 1937–   —Criticism and interpretation. 2. Women and literature—Africa, Southern—History—20th century. 3. South Africa—In literature. 4. Botswana—In literature. I. Title
    II. Series.
PR9369.3.H4Z77   1999
823—dc21
                                         98-55671
                                             CIP

10 9 8 7 6 5 4 3 2 1

Printed in the United States of America

For Sue, who was there from the start
And for Daniel, Matthew, and Jessica, who allowed me to finish

Contents

CONTENTS

Preface

My research into the life and work of Bessie Head began in 1983, when I commenced an M.A. on the writer. My dissertation was one of three under way at the time (I was later to discover), and no full-length study had yet appeared. Indeed, although Head's novels and, to a lesser extent, her stories had attracted their fair share of reviews, and longer pieces had begun to appear, it was really only in the mid-1980s that she became well known internationally and her writings started appearing on universities' lists of prescribed works.

When I completed my study in early 1985, I traveled to Botswana on my way to Zimbabwe with the intention of dropping in on Bessie. Rather naively, I thought that my visit would be taken casually: I'd have an informal chat with her, tell her something about my research and my appreciation of her work, promise to send her a copy of my dissertation, and then leave. I did not know that I was merely the latest in a long line of academic visitors, who by this point were considered unwelcome. Had I known this I certainly would never have had the temerity to approach her little cottage.

As it happened, she was polite and restrained, although she made it clear that an interview was out of the question. She mentioned some of the reasons for her attitude toward academic visitors, spoke a little about her life, and left it at that. I promised to send her a copy of my dissertation and departed. The response I received from her a year later, however, by which time she had received and read my dissertation, was warm and generous, and this indicated to me that although she had learned to steer clear of academics she was still receptive to critical appraisals of her work.

Two months later she was dead. I received a terse telegram from Hugh Pearce, one of her close friends in the last days: "Bessie Head died 17 April to be buried 26 April please inform." Word was already spreading rapidly, and it gradually began dawning on the South African literary community that a bright light had been abruptly extinguished.

In 1986, the year of her death, the first full bibliography on her appeared. Her uncollected writings appeared in two volumes, in 1989 and 1990, and a selection of her letters followed in 1991. A second (vastly expanded) edition of the bibliography was published in 1992, and her previously unpublished early novel and miscellaneous pieces appeared in 1993. In 1995, just under 10 years after her death, the first biography on Head appeared. This body of work is testimony to the growth in stature of this remarkable writer in the last decade.

Some of my own work on Head forms a small part of this growing body of research. I discovered in the late 1980s and early 1990s at various conferences in Europe that she was continuing to attract attention and was fast becoming something of a cult figure. Wherever I went, papers on her were being presented, her works were being taught, and interest in her continued unabated. My own work was partly spurred on by this fervor, and much of it is gathered in the present study.

There are many reasons that the life and work of Bessie Head have attracted such widespread attention. Her life story is one that encapsulates in microcosm the greater social and political evils of the apartheid era in South Africa. The offspring of an illicit alliance between a white woman and a black man, she was in many ways the physical and psychological meeting point of forces that have been in conflict for centuries in Africa: the white colonists who became permanent settlers and the indigenous peoples who bore the impact of the European invasion. In more contemporary terms, she was the physical evidence of racial mingling, a first-generation child of biracial origin born into racist South Africa in 1937.

Because Head was bereft of a secure personal and racial identity, it is little wonder that she came, in her semiautobiographical major novel *A Question of Power,* to locate the battleground of the larger social forces ravaging southern Africa in the psyche of her central character, Elizabeth. Her other work carries within it a similar sense of the psychic stress and moral urgency of a writer trapped in the turbulent currents of her particular time and place. But it is the way in which she bodies this forth in fiction that makes her a perennial source of fascination. Eschewing the overt "protest" mode that came to dominate South African writing of the 1970s and 1980s, she preferred to locate her moral and creative center in individual people, in "how strange and beautiful people can be—just living," as she put it in her social history, *Serowe: Village of the Rain Wind.* And now that the wheel has turned, so much of what was written in such a strident and urgent way in the 1970s and 1980s in South Africa seems dated. The work of Bessie Head has not suffered the same fate.

In a recent SABC radio broadcast on the life and work of Bessie Head, the presenter remarked that "she is a woman who can be known only after death." Notwithstanding all the research that has been done on the life and work of the writer in the last 20 years or more, I would venture the opinion that—like Olive Schreiner, a writer with whom she has been compared—Bessie Head will never be fully known. Like her odd, quirky, highly individualistic works, she will be returned to again and again, but she will remain enigmatic and mysterious.

Chronology

1937   July 6: Bessie Amelia Emery born in Fort Napier Mental Institution, Pietermaritzburg, South Africa, to Bessie Amelia Emery (nee Birch); her father is unknown. Bessie goes into foster care.

1943   Mother dies in mental institution.

1950   Taken out of foster care and placed in Anglican mission orphanage in Hillary, Durban (1950–1956). Attends high school. Trains as primary school teacher.

1956–1958   Works as primary school teacher in Durban.

1958   June: Resigns from teaching; July: leaves Durban for Cape Town; takes up residence in District Six.

1958–1959   Works for *Golden City Post* (newspaper in *Drum* stable).

1959   April: Moves to Johannesburg; works on *Home Post,* weekly tabloid supplement to *Golden City Post.* Meets Dennis Brutus and Lewis Nkosi.

1960   March: The Sharpeville shootings occur; Head is arrested, appears briefly in court, and is released.

1960   April: Attempts suicide; recovers and returns to Cape Town. Meets Harold Head in July, and they marry in September.

1962   May: Howard born. First published piece, a poem entitled "Things I Don't Like," appears in the liberal monthly the *New African.* Continues writing poetry and drafts novella, *The Cardinals.* September: The Heads move to Port Elizabeth, where Harold becomes the first black reporter on the *Evening Post.* They renew their friendship with Dennis Brutus.

1963   The Heads move back to Cape Town; marriage founders. Bessie moves to Atteridgeville, Pretoria, to live with her mother-in-law.

1964   March: Leaves South Africa on exit permit for Serowe, Botswana. Assumes primary-school teaching post.

1965   December: Is blacklisted by education department for desertion of post.

1966   February: Leaves Serowe for Bamangwato Development Association farm at Radisele (80 kilometers south of Serowe); works as typist and does odd jobs. June: Leaves farm after disagreement with committee; moves to Palapye to work as typist with construction firm. August: First major published piece, "The Woman from America," appears in *New Statesman*. Leaves Palapye for Francistown, where she joins refugee community. September: Botswana becomes independent. December: Approached by Simon and Schuster in New York to write novel about Botswana and is given advance of $80.

1968   November: *When Rain Clouds Gather* appears; officially published March 1969 (Simon and Schuster, Gollancz).

1969   January: Moves back to Serowe. March: Has first nervous breakdown; is hospitalized briefly. Builds a house in Serowe, which she calls "Rain Clouds"; joins vegetable garden cooperative. September: Completes *Maru*, commissioned by Simon and Schuster.

1970   December: Onset of serious mental illness.

1971   January: *Maru* published (Gollancz, McCall). April: Has severe mental breakdown and is admitted to mental hospital, Lobatse, south of Gaborone. After three months is discharged. Starts writing *A Question of Power*, drawing extensively on her experiences during periods of illness.

1972   April: Completes *A Question of Power*. The manuscript is rejected by Gollancz, but Davis-Poynter makes an offer in November. Begins historical research on Botswana and begins interviews with Serowe villagers.

1973   November: *A Question of Power* published (Davis-Poynter, Pantheon) to mixed, mostly cautious reviews; publishers enter it for the Booker Prize. Davis-Poynter options the Serowe book. "The Prisoner Who Wore Glasses," which will become Head's most frequently anthologized story, appears in *London Magazine*.

1974   Begins work on the stories that will constitute *The Collector of Treasures*. Completes *Serowe: Village of the Rain Wind* in May and *The Collector of Treasures* (at this stage entitled "Botswana Village Tales") in December.

1976   2–4 April: Delivers paper at writers' workshop hosted by the University of Botswana, her first at an academic gathering. Meets South African writers Mary Benson, Stephen Gray, Sipho Sepamla, and Mbulelo Mzamane.

1977–1978   September 1977–January 1978: Attends International Writing Program at the University of Iowa. October 1977: Learns that her application for Botswanan citizenship has been denied. *The Collector of Treasures and Other Botswana Village Tales* published (Heinemann David Philip).

1979   January: Heinemann accepts *Serowe: Village of the Rain Wind,* ending years of disputes with publishers. February: Granted Botswanan citizenship. 22 June–15 July: Travels to Berlin for Horizons '79 Africa Festival.

1980   Travels to Denmark at invitation of Danish Library Association; delivers short address alongside Kenyan writer Ngugi wa Thiong'o.

1981   June: *Serowe: Village of the Rain Wind* published (Heinemann David Philip).

1982   15–19 June: Attends Second Annual International Conference at the University of Calabar, Nigeria. On the way home, addresses students at University of Zimbabwe.

1983   February: Approached by Ad. Donker, Johannesburg-based publisher, for contribution to series of books by southern African women. Head suggests *A Bewitched Crossroad*.

1984   March: In her last overseas visit, travels to Australia for the Adelaide Festival and appears alongside Bruce Chatwin, Salman Rushdie, Angela Carter, and Andre Brink. May: Enters into an agreement with Heinemann to publish her autobiography, tentatively titled *Living on an Horizon,* in March 1987; nothing comes of this project. October: *A Bewitched Crossroad: An African Saga* published (Ad. Donker).

1985 August: Harold arrives in Botswana to initiate divorce proceedings.

1986 Begins drinking heavily; by April is seriously ill. 17 April: Slips into a coma in Serowe and dies, at age 49, of hepatitis.

Chapter One

Early Life

On 6 July 1937, Bessie Amelia Emery gave birth to her third child, an event that took place at the Fort Napier Mental Institution in Pietermaritzburg, South Africa. The joy that is customary at the birth of a child must have been absent from this event, however. Bessie Emery (nee Birch and nicknamed Toby) had been placed in the institution by her mother after she discovered that Toby was pregnant. Worse was to come after the birth: the infant girl, it was discovered, was "coloured." In the South Africa of this period, an extramarital affair between people of different races not only broke the most entrenched of all social taboos but also was a punishable offense.

Such were the inauspicious beginnings of a woman who was to become one of Africa's most celebrated writers. The years between 1937 and Bessie Head's arrival, in the 1970s, as a writer of note were to contain great hardships and unhappiness for her. Even her success as an international writer of note never entirely enabled her to overcome her false start in life. Dogged by misfortune and mental illness, she was to die a premature death at the age of 49, her literary reputation secure but contentment and happiness finally eluding her.

Bessie Head's story begins much earlier than 6 July 1937. The accident of her conception and birth arose from the personal circumstances of her mother, who married unhappily, witnessed the tragic death of her firstborn son, and endured years of mental illness before her daughter was conceived. Her mother's misfortunes were to have a material effect on the destiny of Bessie Head. Toby was the second of the six children of Walter and Alice Birch, people of tenant-farm English stock who emigrated to South Africa in 1892. Settling initially in Harrismith in the Orange Free State province, where Toby was born on 13 March 1894, they later moved to Johannesburg, where Walter Birch established a successful painting and decorating business.

Toby grew up to be a lively and independent woman; barely a week after coming of age, she announced to her parents that she had married Ira Garfield Emery, an Australian immigrant who worked on the South African Railways. The marriage was destined to be a troubled one. In his family memoir, Kenneth Birch, Toby's youngest brother, points to the couple's fundamental incompatibility: "With her background Toby had prospects, but though outwardly a lively girl, she was actually introspective and a loner. Ira Emery was extrovert, a sportsman with what would today be classified as a good deal of charisma. Their basic attitudes to life were poles apart. They had few friends in common. To the Birchs, sport was a sideshow and amusement."[1]

On 1 December 1915, Toby gave birth to her first child, Stanley. Ira went off to the war in 1916 but returned in 1917, the year in which Walter Birch suddenly died. From 1917 until her death in 1964, Alice Birch was single-handedly to manage the family's affairs, including the increasingly difficult ones of her daughter Toby. Toby and Ira had their second child, Ronald, on 14 February 1919. In that same year, tragedy struck. A taxi carrying businessmen to an East Rand race meeting plowed into the four-year-old Stanley outside the family home in Malvern, Johannesburg, killing him instantly. Toby, who was in the house at the time, heard the sound of the accident and rushed out to find the mangled body of her son. The traumatic event plunged her into a state of deep shock.

In her comprehensive and insightful biography of Bessie Head, Gillian Eilersen correctly argues that "everything that was later to befall [Toby] had its origin in those few minutes on 17 December 1919."[2] From 1931 onward Toby displayed signs of mental agitation and instability and in August 1933 was committed to the Weskoppies Mental Hospital in Pretoria. In September 1934 she was released under the curatorship of her mother. Readmitted in 1935, Toby was discharged toward the middle of 1936, and toward the end of that year she visited her sisters in Durban. In April 1937 it was discovered that she was pregnant. Her mother placed her in the institution where, three months later, she gave birth to the younger Bessie, Bessie Amelia Emery, named after her mother—"the only honour South African officials ever did me," Head was later to remark.[3] Toby never emerged from this institution and died there in September 1943.[4] Provisions were made for Head's education from her deceased mother's modest estate, and the Birch family placed the child in foster care with the Heathcote family of Pietermaritzburg.

The identity of the father of the child to which Toby gave birth six years prior to her death and the circumstances of the conception have never been determined.[5] The Birch family assumed at the time that the newest addition would be white, but when she was returned by a white foster family after just a few days on account of her "strangeness," the notion that Head was fathered by a man of color slowly dawned. She was then placed in foster care for the next 13 years with a Coloured family in Pietermaritzburg.

From this point onward, Head was to have virtually no contact with her white relatives. While Toby was still alive, Head was occasionally visited by her grandmother, but upon Toby's death all personal contact ceased. Alice Birch, remarks her son, "placed an embargo on idle family talk and gossip," but "as she had shouldered the burden and paid the bills of her daughter and her offspring, she decided she had every right to know what was going on" (Birch, 11). Accordingly, she watched over the affairs of her granddaughter from a distance, seeing that she was placed in foster care and seeing to her maintenance and welfare.

The attitudes of Bessie Head's white relatives would now invite condemnation. In 1944, in a letter quoted by Eilersen, Head's half brother Ronald declared that, after the wrapping up of his mother's estate (during which he made over £300 for his half sister's maintenance), "I am having nothing more to do with her" (Eilersen, 10). Alice Birch herself left nothing in her will to her granddaughter, and Kenneth candidly remarks that after Head was placed in an orphanage at the age of 13, his mother, "very experienced in human behaviour, finally turned young Bessie Amelia away from her white relations, the Birch family, and so forced her to make her own way in life, by her own unaided courage, ability and genius" (Birch, 12). From this point until Head's death in 1986, he adds, "not one of Bessie's white relatives ever made any effort whatsoever to countermand their matriarch's disposition, and they all made excuses as to why they did not or could not do so. . . . To the world, and its censure," he concludes, "we abandoned our relation" (12, 17). Indefensible as such attitudes and actions might be, they must be placed in the context of social mores at the time. The combination of mental instability, "permissiveness," and interracial contact made this event a scandal of large proportions in any society, let alone that of white South Africa in the 1930s and 1940s.

Head's life in foster care was not an easy one. The Heathcote family was very poor, a situation aggravated by the death of George Heathcote in 1943. A significant detail to emerge from these years, however, was Head's fascination with reading, an activity her uneducated foster mother, Nellie Heathcote, apparently did not encourage. Nonetheless, Head was later to record that she felt "deeply attached" to the woman she accepted as her mother (*Woman Alone*, 3). In the late 1940s the situation in the Heathcote home deteriorated to the point where the local welfare organization decided to place her in an orphanage.

In January 1950 the 13-year-old Head was taken to St. Monica's Home, an Anglican mission school for Coloured girls located in Hillary, on the outskirts of Durban. The environment was austere and disciplined, with regular punishments meted out for misdemeanors. It was here, however, that Head was to receive an education and some grounding for the lonely and difficult life that faced her.

In December 1951, just under two years after Head began life at St. Monica's, she received another of the many severe jolts in her life. She was told that she would not be going "home" for the holidays, and that the person she regarded as her mother was in fact not her real mother. She was later to recall this calamitous event in the following way:

> I was called to the office of the principal, a British missionary, who announced curtly: "You are not going back to that woman. She is not your mother."
>
> A teacher found me lying prostrate and at the point of collapse under a bush in the school garden. On asking what was the matter, I told her I was about to die as no one would let me go home to my mother.
>
> Thereupon the principal bundled me into her car and for some strange reason raced straight to the Durban Magistrate's Court where a magistrate read something out to me in a quick gabble that I did not hear or understand.
>
> But he looked at me accusingly as though I were some criminal and said, hostilely: "Your mother was a white woman, do you hear?"
>
> On arriving back at the mission, the missionary opened a large file and looked at me with a wild horror and said:
>
> "Your mother was insane. If you're not careful you'll get insane just like your mother. Your mother was a white woman. They had to lock her up as she was having a child by the stable boy who was a native."
>
> The lady seemed completely unaware of the appalling cruelty of her words. But for years and years after that I harboured a terrible and blind hatred for missionaries and the Christianity which they represented, and once I left the mission I never set foot in a Christian church again. (*Woman Alone*, 3 – 4)

The sense of self that Head had held on to so tenuously as a young girl was ripped away from her in this manner. She must for some time have had intuitions that she did not really belong to the foster family, but now she was left with no illusions at all. Not for the last time, she must have felt truly alone in the world.

She did gain from the principal some sense of her true identity, however, as another passage from the reminiscence just quoted reveals:

> But it was also the lady's delight whenever she had a problem with me to open that file and read out bits of it. So I gained a hazy impression of my beginnings, of a pathetic letter written by my mother in the mental hospital, stipulating that above all things, it was her earnest desire that I receive an education and that some of her money should be set aside for my education, of a period of emotional instability and depression in her life that had led her to inflict a terrible disaster on herself.
>
> She had been married and when the marriage fell through she returned to the family home.
>
> In a sudden and quite unpredictable way she decided to seek some love and warmth from a black man. (*Woman Alone*, 4)

That there was also a feeling of liberation buried deep inside the misery of these revelations is reflected in some of the comments Head was later to make. In a letter to Randolph Vigne, she wrote with bleak honesty: "The best and most enduring love is that of rejection."[6] The most that Head could salvage from the wreckage of her life was a sense of existential freedom—a freedom that would never be untrammeled by a sense of intense loneliness and rejection but that nevertheless held out for her the possibility of fashioning some sort of life for herself. Such an impulse manifested itself early in her. At 16, having once again been denied a holiday with Nellie Heathcote, she absconded to her former foster home. During this visit, however, she began to notice the dull conformity that poverty had imposed on the Heathcotes and their neighbors. She remarked in 1975: "They did not dream of enquiring into the riddle of life or attempting to get above it, as I had partly started to do."[7]

She returned to her studies and gained her Junior Certificate in 1953, aged 16. At this time the austere principal featured in the reminiscences previously cited was replaced by the more humane and spontaneous Margaret Cadmore, whom Head was later to memorialize with warmth and humor in her novel *Maru*.[8] Under Margaret Cadmore's leadership, Head flourished in this period. Although her interest in subjects other than English began to wane in the second year of her study for the Natal Teachers' Senior Certificate, a two-year course that qualified her to teach at the elementary school level, she gained the qualification in 1957 and went to teach at a primary school for Coloured children in Clairwood, Durban.

It was during this period that the racial legislation affecting the lives of all South Africans (and those of color in particular) began to be put into effect by the National Party after it had won the fateful general elections of 1948. Emerging from the protected world of a girls-only mission home as an impressionable and sensitive 18-year-old, Head was soon to feel the effects of the racist social program being put into place. The Durban municipal library was reserved for the use of whites only, and she had to resort to joining the M. L. Sultan Library, which was set up by an Indian businessman and open to all races. One immediate consequence of this was her exposure to books on the Hindu religion, to which Head was especially receptive given her desire for knowledge and her negative experiences of Christianity at its austere worst.

Teaching was not Head's ideal vocation: she was not temperamentally suited to the dull routine of the school day and the constant need to discipline her young charges. She resigned from her job in June 1958 and shortly afterward left for Cape Town. Soon after her arrival in the city she wrote to Margaret Cadmore: "I am sorry I could not explain why I left teaching. . . . I was sure and still feel that teaching is not for me."[9]

She moved into the world of journalism, joining the Cape Town office of the *Golden City Post,* a weekly newspaper catering mainly to a black readership. At this time she experienced the insecurity of financial hardship, a condition that was to be her lot for most of her life. In the same letter to Cadmore just quoted, she appealed for financial assistance: "I think perhaps there is some money—about £12 left in Pretoria of what was given me by my mother. Is it possible for me to have it?" (Cadmore 1958a, 2–3). She then went on to remark how much she liked her new job: "The type of stories the Editor sends me out on are sometimes fantastic. A few weeks ago I had to find wives for two lonely bachelors and tomorrow I am taking three crippled children up by cableway to the top of Table Mountain. It's a project of making people's dreams come true" (3–4).

Her characteristic pluckiness is illustrated by the next few lines, in which she remarks that as the only female reporter on the staff, she was given all the stories having to do with mothers or children, whereas the men "get murders and politics. . . .One day," she adds, "I should like to get hold of a good murder" (Cadmore 1958a, 4). In an early reference to her fragile mental state, she notes that another reason she liked the work was that it "leaves no time for mind troubles or frustrations or hysterics" (5). But she concludes, "I am desperately poor. Please help me." And in a canny postscript she appeals for clemency—"I have been wicked to get into this poverty. Don't lecture too much as I'm sorry"—

and plays on her former principal's religious sensibilities: "There was a priest who came to see me (in Durban). He was very nice" (Cadmore 1958a, 5).

This letter contains all of the elements that were later to fall into a familiar pattern: the encounter with economic adversity, the appeal for help from friends, a demonstration of high-spirited tenacity in the face of hardship, and importantly, the shrewd judgment in dropping the right comments to ensure a positive response. In this case, as in many others later, the letter served its purpose. Cadmore responded by sending her £20, and Head wrote an effusive letter of thanks, which also contained another ominous reference to her unstable mental state: "Those two years after I left St Monica's were the most awful years of my life. Owing to my inclination toward Hinduism I went through a mental disturbance that I doubt I could ever stand again."[10] In her youthful exuberance she probably did not anticipate that she would have to endure such disturbances repeatedly in the future and that they would also become more protracted and severe.

She was already realizing just how deep rooted and complicated were the various caste systems in South Africa, however. Remarking that she had had a cool reception from some well-to-do Coloured families on account of her darker color and lack of "class and sophistication," she observes in the same letter that she "detest[ed] snobbery" and "flourish[ed] in the company of an intellectual": "I search avidly for anyone really intelligent. With intelligent people one forgets such shameful matters as the colour of one's skin and facial features which seem to matter so much in South Africa. Heavens! I will not ape anybody. I am an individual. No one shall make me ashamed of what I am!" (Cadmore 1958b, 4). Such defiant resilience carried Head through some difficult times in Cape Town and, later, Johannesburg. She persevered as a cub reporter and after a three-month trial period was appointed a staff reporter, which improved her financial circumstances slightly.

Early in 1959, Head decided to move to Johannesburg. At this time the Defiance Campaign against racist legislation and, in particular, the pass laws began to gain momentum. Although Head's new job (on the *Home Post* supplement to the *Golden City Post*) was innocuous enough— managing a newsletter entitled *Dear Gang* and an advice column called "Hiya Teenagers"—her brief sojourn in Johannesburg in 1959 and 1960 was momentous. Her association with the Pan Africanist Congress (PAC) under Sobukwe, whom she admired and later featured in her story "The Coming of the Christ-Child" (1981), led to her being swept up in the events surrounding Sharpeville in March 1960. Although she was not actually present at the Sharpeville calamity, she did witness Sobukwe's arrest at Orlando police station earlier that day. She was scooped up in the ensuing series of arrests and earned her freedom only by turning state witness. Eilersen reports that in 1972 Head wrote a letter to Sobukwe in which she indirectly apologized for this action (Eilersen, 49).

Most harrowing of all the events that occurred in Johannesburg, however, was Head's first sexual encounter, which Eilersen describes as "a violent and unwelcome one forced upon her" (49). Shortly afterward she attempted suicide for the first time. She survived—painfully—lost her job as columnist on *Home Post,* and returned to Cape Town.

Eilersen notes that Head's job on *Home Post,* which belonged to the same stable as *Drum,* meant that she rubbed shoulders with the likes of Lewis Nkosi, Can Themba, and Dennis Brutus (42). Head was later to retract this presumed affiliation. Questioned more closely by Susan Gardner after their 1983 interview—in which, in one of Head's few instances of name-dropping, she had implied an association with Nkosi, Themba, Es'kia Mphahlele, and Todd Matshikiza[11]—she was compelled to reduce the list of luminaries until she was left with only Lewis Nkosi. Head was later to prove, repeatedly, her ability to face the brutal truth of her troubled life. Her desire, manifested here, to join the mythical *Drum* coterie is one of the few instances of the wistful romanticism that shallowly underlay her gritty realism.

Upon her return to Cape Town she attempted to take up her old reporting job but found that she was unable to and resorted instead to writing and printing a pro-Africanist news sheet called "The Citizen." Unemployed and recovering from her breakdown, she sought friendship in the leftist political circles loosely grouped around the Liberal Party: "The fantastic thing about friendships in South Africa is that one always and only meets one's friends through politics," she later remarked (*Woman Alone,* 15). One of the leading figures of the party in Cape Town, Randolph Vigne, remembers her presence at parties and gatherings vividly: "Bessie was a bright and talkative person, but many found her alarming and feared both her deadly, silent stare of disapproval, and her furious outbursts when her fiercely held Africanist views were offended" (Vigne, 2). In one of her early autobiographical sketches of the period, "Letter from South Africa: For a Friend, 'D.B.,' " Head offers her perspective on these events: "I never joined fundraising campaigns because I can't ask for money. I never paid at fund-

raising parties because I was always broke and yet drank as much wine
as I could and talked as loud as I could and quarrelled with the whites
who were there" (*Woman Alone*, 14).

At this time she met fellow journalist Harold Head, and somewhat
uncharacteristically, it was Bessie who apparently made the first physical
advances. Harold recalls that she stripped naked before him in the darkness of the local community center, at which he was caretaker (Eilersen,
52). James Matthews's later allusion to Bessie's arrival in Cape Town as
"that of a shy mission-reared girl who wrote pastoral poems and wore
cardigans tightly buttoned up to her neck" resonates ironically against
this later revelation.[12] Emotionally, Head tended to be on a "perpetual
rollercoaster" (Randolph Vigne's apt description), and her initial rapture
on meeting Harold clearly constituted one of the highs. (It appears that
after the breakup of her marriage in late 1963, however, she was never
again able to approach sexuality with such forthrightness.[13])

In September 1961 the couple were married in Simonstown, the
small naval town south of Cape Town. Harold secured a job with the liberal new magazine *Contact,* edited by Patrick Duncan, and the pair
moved into a rooming house in District Six. In one of her early sketches
of this period, Bessie vividly portrayed their circumstances:

> The housing situation being what it is, my husband and I were
> immensely grateful to obtain a clean large room to ourselves with a bath-
> room and were prepared to put up with the hazardous and inexplicable
> behaviour of our landlord and landlady. Our landlord was forever threat-
> ening us with bodily assault, ably abetted by our landlady who alter-
> nately suffered from fits of wild generosity and wild anger. One never
> knew where one stood in such a storm-filled atmosphere. I myself am not
> usually very obliging. (*Woman Alone*, 18–19)

The candid last admission is significant: given Bessie's own wild mood
swings, there can be little doubt that at least part of the blame for the
household disturbances could be laid at her door. Despite such domestic
disturbances, however, Bessie was soon pregnant, and Howard was born
on 15 May 1962.

During this period Bessie was writing the "pastoral poetry" alluded
to by James Matthews, the Cape Town–based poet, in his review in July
1969 of Bessie Head's first published novel, *When Rain Clouds Gather.* In
this review Matthews provided some vital information about her early
unpublished writing. Remarking that *When Rain Clouds Gather* "could
not exactly be called the first novel written by Bessie Head, but . . . her

first one published," he went on to allude to her "pastoral poems" and added: "From pastoral poetry she advanced to a short-lived four-page sheet edited by herself" and "wrote a novel while locked up in a hotel room in District Six, living on bread and beer supplied by friends" (Matthews, 9).

The news sheet, "The Citizen," has already been mentioned. The novel, *The Cardinals,* which was first published in 1993, is the subject of discussion in the next chapter. The poetry was until recently thought permanently lost. The only poem Head published in her lifetime was "Things I Don't Like" (which appeared in the *New African* in July 1962), and she soon abandoned the genre.[14] "Things I Don't Like" was Head's first venture into print as a creative writer. Declamatory and full of black consciousness posturings, the poem attests to her anger and frustration at the time. Its antagonistic and confrontational tone, however, is not only sharply divergent from that employed in her later writings but also contrasts markedly with the other poems of the period. The rediscovery of her other early poems is thus also important in demonstrating that "Things I Don't Like" is atypical of Head's writing as a whole.

In 1995 five forgotten early poems were discovered in Cape Town and donated to the National English Literary Museum in Grahamstown.[15] Written in the second half of 1961 and early 1962, they provide invaluable insight into the aspirant writer's early creativity and fill a gap in knowledge about Head's early life in District Six. Head achieved renown as a writer of Botswana, and her writing about South Africa has only become well known since her death.

The five poems—"Self Portrait," "Mr Nobody," "When I Am Thinking of You" (later renamed "Untitled Now"), "Geranium Summer," and "Where the Wind Don't Blow"[16]—are accompanied by an article on the jazz musician Dollar Brand (Abdullah Ibrahim) and a cover letter addressed to the intended recipient of the material (someone she met at a party) in which Head offers some commentary on it. "Against my better judgement," she remarks in this letter, "I have included some of my impetuous writing with certain 'flowery' phrases that I now dislike intensely. I didn't have much choice as the writing I would really like you to read is still in my head." The next two paragraphs are worth giving in full:

> I shall go ahead and apologise for what I don't like. The article on Dollar Brand is slightly hysterical. That is because I was infatuated with him and also slightly dazed at the first meeting. I dislike the hysteria most

intensely. The poetry and stuff is just wild. By that I mean it just came out without effort. The exception is the article typed on pink paper. It pleases me slightly. Though not as much as I would like. I like the poem "Where the Wind Don't Blow." It's the nearest I've come to saying what I really want to say. The "Self Portrait" is what I was like but now with a slightly calmer version.

I don't particularly want you to return the stuff I've sent you. I can't bear to read it and it was just lying in the dust under the bed. I don't mind if you shove it in the nearest W.P.B. when you've finished with it.[17]

There are several noteworthy aspects to Head's remarks. First, it is interesting to note that the nascent writer is extremely critical of what she clearly regards to be juvenilia. That she would prefer her correspondent to read the writing "in her head," however, confirms what is obvious in many of her early articles and sketches: her ambition to be a writer.

Head met Dollar Brand in Johannesburg in March 1960, and it is likely that she drafted the article in typescript with the view to publishing it, although it appears that this never came to be. The "slightly hysterical" nature of the piece is certainly evident in its concluding paragraph: "His challenge is that you have ears that hear his message as an existant [sic], real, refreshing breeze to the soul; as a message of creation from a powerful, vitally alive and creative man. There is no mystery in this. Dollar Brand is as real as the universe!"[18] While there is no doubting the genuineness of her response to Dollar Brand, the piece reveals Head's tendency (evident even in her more mature writing) to eulogize in a way that fails to engage seriously with the subject at hand.

What is noteworthy in Head's comments about the poems is her awareness that the process of writing requires more sustained effort and exertion than she invested in these early attempts. The "article typed on pink paper" is the prose poem originally titled "When I Am Thinking of You" and later simply "Untitled Now." That it "please[d] [her] slightly" is significant in that there are distinct traces here of phrases that would recur in her later writing, particularly *Maru:* "Each day you wake the love is new and new and new"; "the companion of the stars and the moon and the wind and the sun and the sky and the earth and the distant horizon."[19] The third paragraph of the piece—with its spring imagery and half-articulated yearnings for love—strikingly anticipates her early pieces from Botswana, "The Green Tree" (1964) and "For Serowe: A Village in Africa" (1965) in particular.

This is perhaps the most significant aspect of Head's early poetry: its anticipation of her Botswana writings.[20] It is interesting to notice, for example, that her alertness to her natural environment (especially evident in "Untitled Now") did not begin with her arrival in a remote African village. The lines "The earth is a vast space of brown grass—grass and more grass, sweeping out towards the horizon" and "The expanse of cold blue sky and the expanse of hard brown earth are brooding in the cold evening gaze" are of a piece with her descriptions of the flat Botswanan landscape in *When Rain Clouds Gather.*[21]

Her desire to write is also reflected in an early piece entitled "Let Me Tell A Story Now . . ." (first published in 1962), a passage from which reads:

> When anybody asked me this question, namely: "What work do you do?" I used to answer: "Oh, I'm a writer." Which is quite a lie because I've hardly written a thing, and I've tried but I know I just wouldn't be able to earn a living by writing. . . .
>
> When they said: "Oh, that's interesting and what have you written?" I would say: "Well . . . I have two unpublished manuscripts. One got lost in the post. The other got lost among the papers and rubble on a publisher's desk." Nobody believed me, of course, and funnily enough I was telling the truth. (*Woman Alone,* 6)

One of these manuscripts has recently surfaced as *The Cardinals* (1993), a novella that did not find a publisher during her life and which Head sent from Botswana in 1964 as a gift to the poet Patrick Cullinan in gratitude for his help.

In 1962 the Heads moved to Port Elizabeth, where Harold took a job as reporter on the *Evening Post.* Here they reestablished friendship with the poet-activist Dennis Brutus, who, ironically enough, was involved in the Olympic sports movement and was negotiating with Ira Emery (who was general secretary of the South African Olympic Committee) for greater recognition of black sportsmen. Eilersen records the irony of the situation:

> Bessie and Harold, taking a close interest in all these negotiations, did register the fact that "Emery" had also been her maiden name, little realising that Bessie was at that moment extremely close to uncovering the mystery of her identity. Any investigation of Ira Emery's background would have revealed the name of his first wife: Bessie Amelia Emery. The key to Bessie's own life history, which her mother had insisted on stretch-

ing out to her in the form of the shared name, was there for the taking. But Bessie did not realise it. (Eilersen, 59)

In his memoir, Kenneth Birch argues the possibility that Bessie did not wish to trace her white relations: "I do not think my niece was incapable of finding the Birch family. . . . She knew her eldest uncle, Walter (Ben), the then main family representative, was highly unsympathetic, with the implication therefore that the rest of the family were not interested. Bereft of her mother Toby, Bessie became aware that in order to reach her goal she had to go through life unfettered and alone" (Birch, 16).

In support of such an argument, Birch does have Eilersen's own carefully documented details of Head's inability to tackle her autobiography, despite being contracted to write one and even agreeing to a launch date for the proposed volume (Eilersen, 287–89). Whether she was genuinely fearful of having to confront the details of her life unfiltered through the protective lens of fiction or whether she was simply unable to tackle such a large project after the failure of her last work, *A Bewitched Crossroad* (1984), is difficult to determine. Had she really wanted to trace her white forebears, however, there is no doubt she would have been able to do so.

Whatever the circumstances of this ironic turn of events in Port Elizabeth in 1962, Head did not pursue the opportunity to reestablish contact with the Birches, and she and Harold soon returned to Cape Town, where Harold took up the editorship of *Contact*. Bessie was not to remain long in Cape Town this time. On both a personal and a political level, life was becoming untenable. The Group Areas Act of 1950 and its various amendments of the late 1950s and early 1960s were making themselves felt in Cape Town, where plans were under way to clear District Six and remove its inhabitants to the desolate Cape Flats (an event that would occur in 1966, two years after Bessie had left for Botswana). The Treason Trial in early 1961 and the arrest of Nelson Mandela a year later indicated that repression on a national scale had begun in earnest.

An event that touched Head personally was the arrest of Dennis Brutus in 1963.[22] In a letter that appeared at the time, published as "Letter from South Africa: For a Friend, 'D.B.,' " Head mourns the loss of friends and the end of an era: "One is constantly losing friends these days. Some of the refugees, like my friend, 'D.B.,' did not want to leave. Wherever he is now, I know he is unhappy. For those of us who are still here, life becomes lonelier and intensely isolated" (*Woman Alone,* 13). That Head was already contemplating exile is evident from the tone of this letter, published in November 1963. Such sentiments were no doubt hardened by the downward course of her marriage, and toward the end of the year Bessie left Harold and was on her way to Atteridgeville, a township outside Pretoria, to stay with her mother-in-law.

This situation was not to last: Bessie soon fell out with her mother-in-law and by February 1964 had decided that she would try to leave South Africa for good. Her brief association with the PAC prompted the government to deny her a passport, but with the help of Patrick Cullinan she secured an exit permit—which meant that she could leave the country but never return. She applied for, and gained, a teaching position in Serowe in the Bechuanaland Protectorate, and in March 1964, with baby Howard in tow, she began her journey to a new life beyond the borders of a country that had afforded her a childhood and young adulthood of nothing but hardship.

Chapter Two
The Cardinals (ca. 1962)

The posthumous publication in 1993 of Bessie Head's first extended piece of fiction was an event of some importance in the world of South African English literature. Head had long been considered a pioneer and a source of inspiration both for her fellow black South African woman writers (Miriam Tlali, Ellen Kuzwayo, Lauretta Ngcobo, and others) and for those farther afield (Alice Walker, Angela Carter, Nikki Giovanni, Toni Morrison). She achieved this status in the late 1960s and early 1970s with her first three published novels, which were among the earliest novels published by a black African woman writer. The appearance of *The Cardinals* (completed around 1962) set the dates back some six years and demonstrated just how much of a path breaker she was.

The Cardinals shows that Head set herself on the path of being a professional writer very early on, and her considerable successes in this regard testify to a remarkable tenacity. For it was only after the critical acclaim that greeted the appearance of *When Rain Clouds Gather* in 1968 that she was able to call herself a published writer. Her life up to that point was a catalog of hardship and reversals: a doubly illegitimate birth (by racist South African standards), a string of foster families, an early life in the austere religious atmosphere of a mission-run orphanage, a checkered career as a journalist, a failed marriage, and an exit from the land of her birth.

Taken in isolation, *The Cardinals* has a fascination in its own right. A young black woman living in the early 1960s in the fertile milieu of Cape Town's District Six, writing about life in the slum—about politics and sexual prohibitions under apartheid—adumbrating at the same time the more universal incest taboo, and exploring the possibilities of a transcendent love affair: this is a context rich with possibilities, and Head embraces it in her characteristically idiosyncratic and intense manner.

Read in the sequence of Head's oeuvre, *The Cardinals* gives us a side of Bessie Head that we knew little about. Apart from a few early articles, letters, poems, and stories about life in South Africa—which Bessie declared to be an environment that "completely defeated" her as a writer (*Woman Alone,* 62)—the country features in her major fiction

15

only as a baneful shadow presence threatening the fragile initiatives toward racial cooperation among the people it periodically spews across its border.

The themes that *The Cardinals* takes up are recognizable to those familiar with Head's work: the girl protagonist, known successively as Miriam, Charlotte, and Mouse, is abandoned by her mother when her family forces her to give her illegitimate baby to a poor domestic worker. We discover later that Miriam is the issue of a relationship that crosses class and race boundaries (her white mother has a relationship with a Coloured fisherman), and her early life is a blur of shanty-town life, a succession of foster families and neglect. The sole redeeming feature of this uniformly grim childhood is her lessons in literacy from an old man who is the community letter writer. The poignant description of the little girl learning to write her name under the old man's guidance provides the novel with a remarkable beginning and an abiding motif: Miriam writes her way into an identity and a means of existence, a process echoed in Head's own lifelong struggle to give coherence through her writing to the scattered fragments of an emotionally dislocated life.

Deprived of social welfare support on reaching 16 years of age, Charlotte (as she is now known) finds a job with *African Beat,* a scandal sheet posing as a newspaper. Dubbed "Mouse" by her two co-reporters Johnny and James, she enters timidly yet resolutely into the hard-bitten world of sensationalistic journalism. Soon after she arrives at the newspaper she is sent on an assignment with Johnny into the shanty area in which she grew up, and the following exchange occurs:

> "This is where I spent my childhood," she said. "I lived in this shack here."
> The information surprised him. "Very few escape from conditions like this. How did you manage it?"
> "Escape? I don't think I was trying to escape. I wanted to learn to read and write and it did not seem possible if I stayed here."
> He laughed.
> "I think nothing can surprise me, and then life throws up something like you. You have a beautiful soul that was nurtured on a dung heap," he said.[1]

Despite himself, Johnny becomes more and more attracted to Mouse. He is initially unable to reach her in her state of withdrawal but finds a way of accessing her through writing. He gives her the outline of a short story that he is working on and she fills it out. " 'Writing reveals quite a lot about the writer,' " he remarks to her after reading the revised story. " 'This bit here proves to me that you are very much alive inside' " (*Cardinals*, 42).

In a plot twist, we learn about Johnny's past. He was a fisherman, living rough on the beach, muscular and sun-tanned. He attracted the attentions of a mysterious young white woman, who is described as "tall and very thin and walk[ing] in a direct and purposeful way with long, swift strides" (*Cardinals*, 49). In an equally direct and purposeful way she seduced the fisherman:

> For him it was like a high and glorious summer in the bleak winter of his life and for years afterwards the memory of her strange beauty and the hard, vibrating passion of her body lived with him like an unhappiness that could not die. For her it was the tragic responsibility of having destroyed the one thing she had sought from life with a desperate and violent intensity. Devastated and broken, she lay for days half-conscious while her family wondered in shocked silence at her sudden collapse. (*Cardinals*, 54)

The woman becomes pregnant with the fisherman's child but has lost contact with him by then. Her family persuade her to give up the child and to marry a young man who has won their approval. In despair she does so, but on the eve of their departure for another town, where they will marry and start a new life, she commits suicide. The reader now knows what neither Mouse nor Johnny knows: that with the increasing closeness of their relationship, they are in danger of committing incest.

Johnny persuades Mouse to move in with him by saying that he wants to help her with her writing. Mouse accepts but finds that Johnny is soon making demands: " 'There are one or two things I want to get straightened out. I just can't have a woman around who dresses the way you do. Cut two inches off those hems and fix up the slips' " (*Cardinals*, 73). He also tells her that she must learn to cook and " 'do a bit of cleaning up too, and buying things.' " Mouse responds in a way that has become a defensive reflex: "Dazed by the unexpectedness of events, she preferred not to think or feel" (73–74).

Johnny acts in a confusing blend of self-interest and genuine care for Mouse. His disturbingly sexist attitudes—" 'Your legs are quite attractive but you haven't given anyone a chance to look at them. Men like to look at women's legs' "—are offset by some valuable insights that help Mouse unlock her creative potential: " 'I do what I like and I think what

I like. That's what I call inner freedom. It's absolutely necessary for any-one who calls himself, or thinks himself, a writer. You won't be able to think straight in that tight bunched-up state you're in now. You've got to break off the bolts that are keeping you locked up' " (*Cardinals,* 75).

Once she is accustomed to her new surroundings, Mouse is suffused with a feeling of "indefinable happiness" (*Cardinals,* 77). This feeling becomes mixed with a disturbing sense of unease, however, and here we at last encounter squarely the issue that is at the center of the novel. When Johnny gets into her bed the morning after she has moved in, he explains his feelings for her in a way that touches on the theme of incest:

> "You can pretend you're my sister for a bit. Move over. My sister always used to sleep next to me and when I woke in the morning, she'd have her arm tight around me like this. I used to like it. It's a comforting feeling to wake up and find someone with their arm around you. Now that I come to think of it, I must have been a little in love with her too. I used to kiss her, not the way a brother should kiss a sister but the way a man kisses a woman. Like this." (*Cardinals,* 77–78)

This is the second time Johnny evokes the notion of incest in relation to his feelings for Mouse. Earlier, in a conversation with PK, the editor of *African Beat,* he made certain remarks about Mouse that appear to sug-gest a genetic bond between them: " 'It's the inside part, PK. She's got something inside her that agrees with my system' " (65).

That Head is working consciously on the theme of incest is illustrated by an exchange between Johnny and Mouse that follows immediately after his allusion to his relationship with his sister:

> He looked at her with the amused gleam in his eyes. "Do you think there was anything incestuous in that?"
>
> "No," she said.
>
> "I think so. Society would think so too. It would condemn me as unspeakable filth for making love to my own sister. A man like that, it would say, would stop at nothing. He'd even make love to his own daughter. All I can say to society is that it's just as well I have no daugh-ter. I'd probably make love to her too." (*Cardinals,* 78)

Other, earlier passages now begin to take on new significance. In another discussion Johnny has with PK, he remarks that Mouse told him that " 'she started off life in that hell-hole off the National Road.' " He adds that this surprised him, " 'because it's obvious she was not born there' " (27). And shortly afterward he remarks to PK: " 'Everyone knows it's the dumping ground for illegitimate babies. I can only think that that applies in her case' " (28). In a later discussion, this time with James, the latter observes that the scars Johnny is carrying from the past were caused by a woman: " 'The fact that you've been messing up high-society bitches proves that it was one of them who gave you the knock' " (46). "Messing up" women, in James and Johnny's parlance, means getting them pregnant. The possibility, then, that Johnny "messed up" a "high-society bitch," that this woman "dumped" her baby at the "hell-hole," and that this baby was Miriam/Charlotte/Mouse is clearly being suggested here. Somewhat ominously, both PK and James try to prevent Johnny from falling in love with Mouse. PK says to Johnny: " 'All I know is that you're dangerous. I just feel sorry for that poor kid. She doesn't know what's coming to her' " (30). And James says to him: " 'Why don't you leave the kid alone? She's half crazy already. It just needs someone like you to mess her up and she'll go round the bend completely' " (46).

All of this suggests that the author is attempting to play on the many ironies inherent in the situation. There is a more important issue here, however: to what extent is Johnny aware that his relationship with Mouse might be an incestuous one? Another, even more serious issue lies beyond this: to what extent is Head attempting to make a case for the redemptive power of an incestuous relationship in an abnormal society like that of South Africa in the 1950s and 1960s?

In *The Cardinals* Head constructs a variant of the Oedipus Rex myth in which an unwitting father-daughter (rather than mother-son) relationship is entered into. This is not the difference that is at issue here, however; instead, whereas the classical myth registers the deep sense of horror and revulsion at what has happened (Jocasta hangs herself and Oedipus blinds himself), which serves to reinforce the incest taboo, *The Cardinals* appears to suggest that an incestuous relationship might well be curative and beneficial.

Having introduced Mouse to the idea of an incipiently incestuous relationship with his sister, and having noted that she is neither shocked nor outraged, Johnny goes on to present to her details about their family background in a way that suggests that a sympathetic interpretation of the relationship between him and his sister is being solicited:

> "After my father died my mother kept on getting children from various men. There were about twelve of us altogether. She was nearly always drunk too, so we just grew up like a lot of animals. My sister was a pros-

titute at the age of ten. She was the eldest in the family and only did it so
that we could have food to eat. She never complained, but at night she
used to come and lie next to me and cry. One night she was stabbed to
death. I think I would have never forgiven myself if I had withheld the
kind of love she wanted from me. All that just makes me not care one
hell about the laws and rules of society. They are made by men and
women who know nothing about suffering. I had many reasons for asking you to come and live with me. You are the only person I can bear to
have near me now. I can't take the sham and hypocrisy and false values
any longer." (*Cardinals,* 78)

The reasons for Johnny's sister being a prostitute are graphically rendered, and we are encouraged to understand and accept her for what she
does. But this is only one part of the appeal being made here. The more
important point is that she came to Johnny for the love that her parents
and her society have denied her, and it is clear that "the kind of love she
wanted" from Johnny was at least partially incestuous. The palpable gap
in the text between "she used to come and lie next to me and cry" and
"One night she was stabbed to death" represents the unsayable: that "the
kind of love" between her and Johnny was not that which usually obtains
between brother and sister. The "laws and rules of society" to which
Johnny then alludes are clearly those concerning incest, and these we are
encouraged to see as "sham and hypocrisy and false values." A powerful
case for acceptance—or at least condoning—of incest is being made here.
The idea of men taking advantage of a 10-year-old girl's poverty to
indulge their pedophiliac tendencies is being weighed implicitly against
the healing (albeit incestuous) love between a brother and sister.

If a case can be made for an incestuous relationship between a
brother and sister in these circumstances, what about an incestuous relationship between father and daughter if the circumstances also justify it?
Johnny has made Mouse aware that the relationship between him and
his sister was not "normal." He then goes on to say that if he had a
daughter he would "probably make love to her too," and asks Mouse:
"Does that shock you?" (*Cardinals,* 78). Her no signifies that they have
reached an understanding that societal norms are not universal, transcendent imperatives that must be obeyed unquestioningly. Each is prepared to entertain the idea that under certain circumstances the incest
taboo justifiably can be transgressed. "*The Cardinals,*" the author notes
on a prefatory page, "in the astrological sense, are those who serve as the
base or foundation for change." Is the suggestion here that Mouse and

Johnny are the cardinals that serve as the foundation for a very radical kind of change?

In the end the author does not develop these possibilities. Having flirted with the idea of making Johnny at least dimly conscious that the relationship into which he is entering is incestuous, she retreats from the consequences of pursuing this possibility and provides a more conventional ending. The element of risk and danger is not entirely effaced, however: at the novel's conclusion we see Mouse and Johnny on the cusp of transcendence and oblivion, as they contemplate a relationship fraught with dangers known and unknown (principal among the latter being the incestuous nature of their relationship). Says Johnny: " 'Life is a treacherous quicksand with no guarantee of safety anywhere. We can only try to grab what happiness we can before we are swept off into oblivion' " (*Cardinals*, 137).

The incest theme is not the only area in which the novel falters. Evidence of the author's youthfulness are present in certain formal attributes of the text—the stilted and callow dialogue, the sometimes sketchy characterization, and the bewildering and unaccountable mood swings in the main characters. Another area of weakness is Mouse's behavior. Like Margaret in *Maru,* Mouse is passive and inert—a tendency she shares with some of Head's other female protagonists and that feminist critics have found disturbing. Here we have character as palimpsest, a slatelike surface on which assertive male characters inscribe their wills without, however, ultimately being able to penetrate (Mouse remains both passive and chaste until the very end). The mutations in her name (all of which she accepts unquestioningly) are the most obvious example of this. Her passive acceptance of Johnny's bullying is less easy for the reader to accept, and the close juxtaposition of love and violence in his behavior toward Mouse is very disturbing.

In defense of her passivity it can be said that her identity and sense of self are in a constant state of evolution—a state common to most young adults perhaps, but one that is especially acute in the case of a person utterly bereft of the orienting matrices of a family history. Mouse inherits the double-edged sword that is existential freedom, but she experiences only too painfully the sharp edge of loneliness, disorientation, and fathomless anxiety. All of this makes her an easy target for Johnny's aggression. Nonetheless, that she is never able to evolve beyond being the hapless victim of another's manipulations makes her an ambiguous heroic figure.

There is an emotional urgency that the reader feels in the text, however, and this redeems the novel to a certain extent. This urgency stems from the author's intense anger at the laws that (then) forbade sexual union between members of different racial groups. The Prohibition of Mixed Marriages Act of 1949 made marriages between whites and members of other racial groups illegal. Earlier, the Immorality Act of 1927 had prohibited extramarital intercourse between whites and Africans, and this act was amended in 1950 to include members of the other nonwhite racial groups as well. As a first-generation "Coloured" born of an illicit relationship between a white woman and a man of color, Head was only too painfully aware of how she was viewed by the bureaucrats and practitioners of apartheid. Margaret Daymond sums up the issue well. The provisions of the Immorality Act, she remarks, "must have brought about the fusion of personal fears and political angers which is evident in *The Cardinals.* The individual rejection that Bessie Head had suffered as a child . . . was now being matched by the annihilating rejection of a whole people that was implicit in the legislation. Its prohibitions were sexual, so that the very union which had produced her was now a criminal act; but they were also existential, so that people like Bessie Head must have felt that their right to exist was being called into question."[2]

As with all of Head's work, *The Cardinals* leaves the reader bewitched, unsettled, and baffled. The setting outwardly may be District Six on the eve of the Sharpeville massacre, but Head draws the reader insistently into the psychospiritual domain that would form the battleground of her novelistic tour de force, *A Question of Power.* Read against the background of this later semiautobiographical work, *The Cardinals* reveals the 25-year-old author visiting the ghosts of a shadowy personal history (illicit love, rejection, madness, tragedy)—a process that prefigures the larger-scale novelistic explorations to come. Although it is flawed and unresolved, *The Cardinals* leaves the overall impression of raw power and mystery.[3]

Chapter Three

In Exile in Botswana

Eilersen characterizes the 1964–1977 phase of Head's life as "a fresh start" (Eilersen, 63). With hindsight, however, it is possible to see that Head's false start in life was never to be overcome. According to Head herself, she lost the teaching job for which she traveled to Botswana largely as a consequence of sexual harassment. The principal of the school apparently thought that "he could get started to sleep with [her]" (Vigne, 10). Not succeeding, he allegedly turned on her and manhandled her in front of the schoolchildren. Head claims that she then bit his arm to free herself and "fled away from the school, screaming." This was the second time she had left the school in this fashion, and the school committee requested that she undergo a medical examination to assess her mental state. She refused, and in December 1965 the Department of Education blacklisted her on the grounds of dereliction of duty.

Without employment, and under a cloud after this debacle, Head turned to writing in all earnestness. Up to this point she had published several mostly autobiographical pieces for the *New African* (which was itself now in exile in London). She reestablished contact with its editor, Randolph Vigne, and this proved crucial to her survival in the lean years before the publication of *When Rain Clouds Gather.* Along with the moral support he provided regularly in his letters, Vigne offered Head a publication outlet (and small but vital payments) for her essays and sketches.

With Serowe for the moment an impossible place in which to live and work, Head went 80 kilometers south to the small town of Radisele, where she began work as what she called an "odd job man" on the Bamangwato Development Association farm (Vigne, 28). Apart from doing some typing, she participated in crop production, notably the harvesting of Turkish tobacco (a detail that finds its way into *Rain Clouds*). She had intuitions that the situation would not last, however, and that she would have to become more reliant on her writing: "The one snag about the farm is that it is also run by the same men as the school committee." She astutely adds: "A good book, published, may be an open sesame to more creative, constructive work" (Vigne, 21).

By the middle of 1966 she was once again without employment and a place to live. What follows is Eilersen's moving description of how Head lost her job at the Bamangwato Development Association farm at Radisele:

> At the end of June, five months after arriving there, she left the farm hurriedly. The committee who ran it had had many complaints about the fact that she and Howard were living in the visitors' rondavel. A confrontation resulted and Bessie was thrown out. This time there was no one to whom she could turn. She took the bus as far as Palapye. With her bundles and boxes, she settled down on the steps of the little post office. Her four-year-old boy, tired and bewildered, pressed himself against her.
>
> She was homeless and desperate. Sitting there, Bessie penned a plea to Randolph [Vigne] to help her in whatever way he could. "It would be a relief to be free of malice, intrigue and unfathomable, weird, weird people who are shockingly cruel," she said in her short note. But she was not completely broken, for she concluded: "I'm holding on." (Eilersen, 85)

The elements of this episode—confrontation, eviction, and the ensuing loneliness and desperation—repeated themselves with numbing regularity in Head's later life. And now, with no money, no friends, no family, no home, no job, and no country that wanted to claim her, Head—not for the last time—began to make plans for leaving Botswana.

It is one of the central ironies of Bessie Head's story that she became the world-acclaimed writer from a country that denied her citizenship for 15 of the 22 years she lived there. It is a further irony that she spent most of those 22 years trying to get out of the country. Kenya, Nigeria, Zambia, India, Britain, Norway, Germany, and Canada were some of the destinations Head feverishly and ineffectually pursued while writing such eulogies as "For Serowe: A Village in Africa" (1965).

After her eviction from the farm at Radisele, Head worked for a short while as a typist for a construction firm in Palapye. This job did not last long either, however, and for reasons that begin to sound familiar. "Can't explain except that the circumstances were very sordid," she wrote to Vigne. "Seems if I decide to sleep with every Tom, Dick and Harry—I'll keep a job" (Vigne, 38).

At about this time, however, a piece dating from her days in Serowe was accepted for publication, and this was to prove decisive for her career as a writer. It was the autobiographical sketch "The Woman from America," which appeared in the British *New Statesman* in August 1966 (and is reprinted in *A Woman Alone,* 31–36). This was her first major piece for an important international magazine. The article was read by an editor for Simon and Schuster in New York, who prompted her to write a novel and gave her an advance of $80 to buy writing materials (Vigne, 46). *When Rain Clouds Gather* was the ultimate result, but Head would endure three years of hardship as a refugee before seeing the book in print.

For the moment she had to find a place to live, and without a passport or employment she was forced to join the refugee community at Francistown, in northeast Botswana. Located close to both the Rhodesian and Zambian borders, Francistown was ideally positioned for refugees looking for a gateway to the north. For Head, however, Francistown provided an opportunity to gather her resources and begin writing a novel.

By January 1967 she had completed the first two chapters of *Rain Clouds,* and she wrote steadily from that point onward. By the end of the year the novel was entirely drafted, although it took another full year to complete. She received her first copy early in 1969 and instinctively must have realized what it could mean to her, for she wrote to Vigne: "God, God, God but it looks terrific. I feel this way because it is only a first baby. I am going out of my mind" (Vigne, 81).

Shortly afterward Head returned to Serowe and placed Howard in Swaneng Primary School. Swaneng was one of the many projects initiated by Patrick van Rensburg, the former South African diplomat who had broken ranks by leaving South African government service and going into exile in Botswana to start self-help projects. Van Rensburg was one of Head's most important pillars of support in Serowe. Through the years he would help her by raising grants, supporting her applications for scholarships, and most important, looking after Howard when she was too ill or unable to do so herself.

Such an occasion arose shortly after she returned to Serowe. Head was evicted from the house she was renting and had to ask Van Rensburg to look after Howard until she was properly settled. She also very soon began to encounter the renewed animosity of the Serowan villagers. Apparently rumors started circulating that she was being supported by a man who visited her secretly at night. She believed that people invented the story to explain the fact that she survived without any visible means of support (Vigne, 82–83).

It was this kind of hostility that provoked the first of her serious mental disturbances, in late March 1969. "It is painful to me," she wrote to Randolph Vigne, "that what I built up and suffered for and

dreamt about has left me with very little dreams and visions at present."
Adding that *Rain Clouds* was "all in vain" because there was "such a
black, bitter and violent rage" in her heart, she goes on to describe the
circumstances of her nervous breakdown:

> I sometimes can't look at the face of a black man or woman without at
> the same time thinking that they are the epitome of all that is grasping,
> greedy, cruel, back stabbing and a betrayal of all that is good in
> mankind. Half of this was that I had to be admitted to hospital with a
> nervous breakdown. Half of it was this village. I came here because of the
> school. It is still the school that keeps me here but I really live on some
> swinging pendulum with a very precarious mental balance. (Vigne, 85)

The breakdown was precipitated by severe insomnia and nights of con-
tinuous nightmares filled with voices taunting her for being a "Bushman dog" (Vigne, 86). Out shopping one day with Howard, she suddenly began screaming. She was admitted to a hospital and heavily
sedated. The rest worked wonders: she emerged from the hospital soon
afterward, calm and apparently recovered. This recovery, however, was
never to be a full one. Although her nightmares subsided for a while,
her deep mistrust of local people was never entirely eradicated. A little
later she remarked to Vigne that she was not able to "endure the sight
and face of a black man or woman any longer," and that "maybe God is
just as evil and malicious as these people and long planned my destruction" (Vigne, 86).

At about this time *Rain Clouds* was officially published in New York,
and reviews started pouring in. They were generally favorable and must
have been some comfort to her in her reduced state. The appearance of
her first novel also opened up the world to her: people in the literary
world suddenly became aware of this earnest young woman writer of
Botswana, and correspondence between her and editors of magazines
and publishing houses soon began.

One of these individuals was Ann Stephenson, an editor of juvenile
fiction at Simon and Schuster (the original publisher of *Rain Clouds*),
who commissioned her to write a book "something like *Catcher in the
Rye,* of 30,000 words" (Vigne, 97). By August 1969 Head had completed a draft of the book, which she described as "a sizzler, full of illegitimate children." She was incensed by Simon and Schuster's projection
of her as a children's book writer and reacted by writing a book that
would challenge this label: "Why can't they let me alone, just as a
writer?" (Vigne, 97).

While she awaited a response she began building a house with the proceeds of the paperback sales of *Rain Clouds*. "The house is minute but the pride is overwhelming," she remarked to Randolph Vigne (Vigne, 98). She was already beginning to enjoy the benefits of being a published writer, and the little house "with two rooms, and a third divided into bathroom, toilet and kitchen" (Vigne, 98) was to provide her with a stable center in an otherwise turbulent and insecure life.

Simon and Schuster turned down *Maru*, but it was quickly picked up by Gollancz in London and appeared early in 1971. As Eilersen astutely observes: "For the second time running, a novel had been almost snatched out of her hands by a publisher. As yet, she did not realise what an achievement this was" (Eilersen, 114). Head was to realize, as the seventies wore on, just how difficult it was to make her way as an unconventional writer based in a remote village in Africa. *A Question of Power* (1973), widely regarded as her major work, sold so poorly that the publisher (Davis-Poynter) lost money and refused to purchase paperback rights. The minor success of Head's admirable collection of stories, *The Collector of Treasures* (1977), was overshadowed by her struggle to publish *Serowe: Village of the Rain Wind* (1981), a work she regarded as far more important. The last work to appear in her lifetime, *A Bewitched Crossroad* (1984), was taken up by a local publisher (Ad. Donker in Johannesburg) and never made it into paperback.

For the moment, however, Head was preoccupied with the building of her house (appropriately dubbed "Rain Clouds") and moving in late in 1970. She also became involved in something else that was to provide an anchor in her life: cooperative vegetable gardening. Her partner, Bosele Sianana, spoke a little English (Head herself spoke no Setswana), and the two for many years would toil mutely in the enervating Botswana sun, providing themselves with a little income and Head with a therapeutic activity that proved critical to her psychological survival.

Indeed, her mental state at this time was far from stable. "I live on a huge assortment of tablets," she remarked to Vigne, adding: "The truth is I just often feel severely ill and I don't know what's wrong myself" (Vigne, 103). She became obsessed with the notion that Seretse Khama, Botswana's president, was both God and the devil at once. In the nightmares she was having at the time, which are recounted graphically in *A Question of Power,* Seretse (given the name Sello in the novel) takes on both guises. There can be little doubt that she was approaching complete insanity. Her "slow churning agonies" were wearing her down to the point where she was unable to keep her inner torture to herself

(Vigne, 108). In a dramatic outburst, she struck her well-meaning and kindly neighbor Mrs. Blackmore on the side of the face and unleashed a torrent of abuse on the hapless old woman. Mrs. Blackmore had apparently provoked Head's ire by showing concern for her in her worsening condition and expressing what appeared to Head to be conventional Christian pieties that only mocked her in her abject state.

This heralded the beginning of a complete mental collapse. Early the next morning Head went to the village post office and put up a signed notice declaring that Seretse Khama had committed incest with his daughter and had concealed the fact that he had murdered his vice president, Quett Masire (another of Head's unfounded obsessions). Later that day two policemen came to her house and arrested her. She appeared before a magistrate and was completely incoherent; the magistrate ordered that she be admitted to the hospital. The doctor there soon realized that her problems could be treated only with psychiatric care and arranged for her to be transferred to the country's only mental hospital, at Lobatse, south of the capital, Gaborone.

For three months Head languished in the hospital. She was initially very aggressive and uncooperative and only later became more friendly and helpful, which secured her release. She returned to Serowe in late June and fired off a letter to Vigne, in which she baldly stated, "I've just got home. I was locked up in a loony bin for nearly 3 months" (Vigne, 142). She added that she had "lived in a sort of nightmare . . . for so long" and that by the end of 1970 she was "so broken" that she "could hardly walk." She was clearly embarrassed by her earlier behavior and wild accusations, for she did not go into any detail about them, saying only in a later letter that the "things I said and did at the time were a kind of final howl. They were so bad that I cannot repeat them" (Vigne, 143).

Her letters to another regular correspondent at the time reveal the full horror of what she lived through. Dorothea Ewan was an English teacher at Swaneng Hill School from 1969 to 1971 and was in close contact with Head during this time. The two continued to correspond for some years after Ewan returned to South Africa in 1972. Dorothea Ewan lodged nine letters from Bessie Head with the National English Literary Museum in Grahamstown in 1991. The first is dated 30 September 1972, the last 15 December 1974. The fascination of this period is that it straddles two distinct phases in Head's life. She was emerging gradually from the horror depicted in *A Question of Power* and moving into the more tranquil period that spawned *The Collector of Treasures* and

Serowe: Village of the Rain Wind. A Question of Power is the pivotal work in this sequence, encompassing as it does Head's autobiography, mixed in with her contemporary life in Serowe and her ruminations in more general terms on politics, religion, and interpersonal relationships.

In the first letter (dated 30 September 1972) Head remarks: "My book [*A Question of Power*] was rejected by my American publishers but Heinemann still want to print it except that they say it is rather inaccessible and want cuts and re-writing and re-organising of chapters."[1] She also expresses a desire to get to the bottom of things, regardless of the emotional cost involved—a desire that is strongly reminiscent of the impulse behind *A Question of Power*. With respect to what she calls "terrible deep brooding on life," she remarks: "Why, if it causes so much anguish, the roots of that anguish have to be pulled out and examined" (Head 1972, 2). This clearly expresses an important motivation for writing *A Question of Power:* her desire to exorcise personal demons.

Strong overtones of *A Question of Power* are also present in the second letter (dated 28 January 1973): "You know when one wades through hell, it asserts its ways. You have to watch every detail. Later you form your conclusions, when you have a grasp of the situation."[2] Throughout the novel itself there is an undertone of horror about life in Botswana that Head suppresses rather successfully. It is likely that she had to do so to preserve her dream of her rural haven, her writer's niche. In her letters, however, she gives full vent to these feelings: "When I think of the horror of my own life, the deeds of South Africa are innocent evil. I have never known greater horror of soul than what I lived through in Botswana."[3] She reports that a friend's horror at what she experienced in South Africa issued in the precept that one should "treat people gently." Head observes: "I have been so shocked by my life in Botswana that I came to a similar conclusion" (Head 1973a, 1). In attempting to externalize her inner torture, she shifted her horror and anxiety (about her own self-worth, statelessness, poverty, isolation) onto real personae, especially political figures—hence her wild allegations involving Seretse Khama and Quett Masire.

In her fifth letter to Dorothea Ewan (dated 9 August 1973) Head exultantly announced that *A Question of Power* would be published on 29 October 1973: "Davis-Poynter Ltd, my publishers, have raised the book to the skies."[4] But in the next sentence a tone of irony enters: "They like it immensely, so they say" (Head 1973b, 1). Even before the book appeared, then, Head seemed ready to go on the defensive, or to adopt an ambivalent attitude toward the book.

In her seventh letter (dated 27 December 1973) Head refers to Ewan's help in reading and commenting on the typescript of *A Question of Power* and then remarks: "Actually, the whole story fills me with great sorrow and disillusion—my conclusions are triumphant but my experience was thoroughly evil."[5] This is an indication that although completing the book was a vindication of her inner strength and will to survive—and was also no doubt therapeutic—she was, finally, never able to put the experience entirely behind her. *A Question of Power* may have a triumphal ending, but sorrow and disillusionment clearly accompanied its completion.

Indeed, the optimism the protagonist expresses at the novel's close may have been forced. Head was determined to fashion an idealized retreat, a place of refuge after the ravages of her life in South Africa, but her fear and hatred of narrow tribalism and of the perceived nepotism and greed of Botswana's political leaders are ever present in her letters. One example is a comment that closes her seventh letter to Dorothea Ewan: "I'm operating on my last legs—frankly this country terrifies me more that [*sic*] I've ever been terrified in my life before. When one looks back at a life of blunders, I wish to undo only one blunder, the decision to build a little home in Serowe—it was as though howling hell itself tore at me when I decided to stay here and where the hell could I go?" (Head 1973c, 1).

Clearly, *A Question of Power* had a purgative function, and this is why it is so explicit and extreme. By externalizing—making public—her inner torment she hoped to put distance between her and her demons. And this process, by its very nature, would permit no half-measures. That Head had at least partially exorcised her personal demons is suggested by the fact that she was never again to have as dramatic and complete a collapse as occurred in the first half of 1971. She had also found a publisher for *A Question of Power,* and although the book was never to sell well and she was to remain insecure about its reputation for the rest of her life, she was now at least able to look a little more steadily at the world around her.

Chapter Four
When Rain Clouds Gather (1968)

In the opening pages of *When Rain Clouds Gather,* Makhaya Maseko, a young black South African political refugee, flees across the border to Botswana to leave behind one part of Africa that he considers to be "mentally and spiritually dead."[1] His flight into exile is prompted by the iniquities of the South African political system, which he felt impelled to resist. His resistance led to a two-year jail sentence. The disintegration of self that resulted from his experience of black urban ghetto life in South Africa he carries with him on his flight to Botswana. The novel, then, is a record of a South African political exile's determination to take root in a foreign land.

There are aspects of *When Rain Clouds Gather* that point to Head's latent skepticism very early on. Makhaya's name, to begin with, has an ironic resonance: "Makhaya" translates roughly from the Zulu as "one who stays home" (*Rain Clouds,* 9). And his very penetration into Botswana is accompanied by the warning that he is running on "to whatever illusion of freedom lay ahead" (7). Botswana does not unambiguously represent a haven of peace and fulfillment, and before Makhaya even crosses the border he has his first taste of the conservative tribalism of the region. The old man who gives him shelter remarks: " 'We Barolongs are neighbours of the Batswana, but we cannot get along with them. They are a thick-headed lot who think no further than this door' " (10).

Once across the border, Makhaya encounters a suspicious old woman who grudgingly sells him shelter for the night and offers him her young granddaughter. Already Head has presented the reader with critical problems in southern African society. The old man is an exponent of the sort of reductive politics that conceptualize the South African conflict in simplistic racial terms: the white man, he believes, is the "only recognized enemy of everyone" (*Rain Clouds,* 10). He also opposes education—" 'It's only the education that turns a man away from his tribe,' " he remarks to Makhaya (9)—and espouses tribalism of the narrowest sort, as exemplified in his remarks just quoted. The old woman, for her part, is mean and unscrupulous, and yet her plight is sympathetically rendered. Makhaya astutely observes that she has probably spent years eking out a frugal existence and that she is also a victim of male domination in traditional tribal life. Child prostitution here also becomes an indictment of male domination. So entrenched is the notion of man as "nothing more than a grovelling sex organ" (15) that Makhaya's rejection of the sexual offer is interpreted as the workings of a deranged mind. The old woman is astonished at Makhaya's behavior: " 'I have not yet known a man who did not regard a woman as a gift from God! He must be mad!' " (15). Head clearly uses the figure of the old woman as an indictment of the sexism inherent in tribal society and, at the same time, of the poverty and oppression the destruction of tribal life creates.

The description of Botswana in the first part of the novel therefore reflects the ambivalence in Head's response to the country. The idyllic setting of the old woman's hut is undercut by her shrill voice and manipulative ways. The rhythmic tinkling of the cowbells that Makhaya hears after he has crossed the border contains a similar ambivalence: do they herald a new way of life, of harmony after so much discord, or are they ominous—evocative of witch doctoring and "ghoulish rites by night" (*Rain Clouds*, 11)?

The opening passages of the novel also contain some lyrical descriptions of the Botswanan landscape: "Here the land was quite flat, and the sunshine crept along the ground in long shafts of gold light. It kept on pushing back the darkness that clung around the trees, and always the huge splash of gold was split into shafts by the trees. Suddenly, the sun sprang clear of all entanglements, a single white pulsating ball, dashing out with one blow the last traces of the night. So sudden and abrupt was the sunrise that the birds had to pretend they had been awake all the time" (*Rain Clouds*, 16). This is a characteristic description of Botswana by Head. It is lyrical as well as wry. The inner lives of the birds are infused with a human significance. The birds themselves are seen to possess the human qualities with which humankind seeks to fill the universe. Coinciding with this romantic impulse, however, is Head's awareness of the harshness of Botswana. This ambivalence is reflected succinctly in her description of Botswana as "bewitchingly beautiful" (17). This phrase strikingly anticipates the problems that beset the heroine Elizabeth in *A Question of Power* when she grapples with the demons that assail her nightly from within the seemingly tranquil Botswana environment.

Makhaya's reasons for leaving South Africa are fundamentally political, yet his exile is not part of an overt political strategy. He feels too disintegrated to launch a fresh offensive against South Africa from across the border. Instead, he is determined simply to draw a curtain on his South African past and begin again elsewhere. Before he crosses the border he remarks to the old man: " 'I just want to step on free ground. I don't care about people. I don't care about anything, not even the white man. I want to feel what it is like to live in a free country and then maybe some of the evils in my life will correct themselves' " (*Rain Clouds,* 10). This characterizes Head's own attitude to exile. In an early sketch she says of Serowe, her adopted home: "Somehow, by chance, I fled to this little village and stopped awhile. I have lived all my life in shattered little bits. Somehow, here, the shattered little bits began to come together" (*Woman Alone,* 30).

Makhaya's quest is for "peace of mind," which he opposes to the road that leads to "fame and importance" (*Rain Clouds,* 20). This is a typical Bessie Head polarity. On her novels she remarked: "I would deliberately create heroes and show their extreme willingness to abdicate from positions of power and absorb themselves in activities which would be of immense benefit to people" (*Woman Alone,* 73). Characters in her later novels make similar choices. She is clearly skeptical of political activism, and her characters seem instead bent on pursuit of personal fulfillment. They strive to unite their interior lives with the exterior world. In *When Rain Clouds Gather,* Golema Mmidi, the village to which Makhaya flees, is the ideal site for this unification.

Golema Mmidi is full of individuals who have fled there "to escape the tragedies of life" (*Rain Clouds,* 22). The village claims its name from the occupation of its inhabitants—crop growing. It is a place inhabited by people determined to make a fresh start in life and to survive. Their harsh circumstances have forced them to become progressive: without any traditionally acquired wealth, they have been impelled to break with traditional agricultural practices and to experiment with new methods. Head is interested in this sort of people. They represent possibilities for a new life, something she herself was desperately trying to reconstruct: "Botswana was a traumatic experience to me and I found the people, initially, extremely brutal and harsh, only in the sense that I had never encountered human ambition and greed before in a black form" (*Woman Alone,* 68).

Greed in a black form is what Makhaya encounters in Matenge, the viciously exploitive and perverse subchief of Golema Mmidi. The unconventional villagers with whom Makhaya comes to ally himself pose a threat to Matenge: in their break with tradition they implicitly question his right to rule over them. Tradition no longer has answers to starvation, poverty, and human misery, and the villagers of Golema Mmidi are prepared to explore the option of modernity. Toward the end of the novel, this option is labeled "the progress of mankind" (*Rain Clouds,* 145).

Matenge is malicious and reactionary. He uses his servants as personal slaves and enforces the rigid class distinction between royalty and commoner. Flanked by the semiliterate Pan-Africanist Joas Tsepe, Matenge becomes a force for evil in the novel. Pitted against this unholy alliance between die-hard traditionalism and opportunistic black nationalism are the progressive characters in *When Rain Clouds Gather:* Gilbert Balfour, a young English agronomist; Dinorego, who meets Makhaya first and brings him to the village; and Paulina Sebeso, a passionate and lonely widow exiled from her home in northern Botswana. Maria—Dinorego's daughter—and Mma-Millipede, with her quaint blend of Christianity and Setswana custom, are two lesser characters who join the four main protagonists in their bid to oppose Matenge and the weight of tradition behind him. The villagers of Golema Mmidi are described as "a wayward lot of misfits" (*Rain Clouds,* 23), yet led by Makhaya and Gilbert, Paulina and Dinorego, they work for an alternative to starvation and suffering. They break with tradition and are thus able to forge a new future for both Golema Mmidi and, the novel seems to imply, ultimately the whole of Botswana.

Makhaya's meeting with Gilbert is like a union of kindred spirits: "There was the kind of defiance in the man Gilbert that found an echo in his own heart" (*Rain Clouds,* 26). Gilbert himself is an exile, in flight from the stifling life of upper-class England. His kind of exile, however, is very different from Makhaya's. He is escaping from bourgeois orderliness, from a kind of life that contains no challenges for an energetic and adventurous young man. Makhaya is escaping the total disintegration of self threatened by racial oppression. Yet both feel the need to engage with the world in a constructive way, to make inroads into poverty and oppression rather than succumb to predestined styles of life: Makhaya a submissive servant of the white overlord, Gilbert a victim of the stultifying rigidity of a class-stratified society. What unites them is their loneliness, their social alienation, and also their desire to integrate their inner needs with their outer realities. Being closer to African tribal society, Makhaya can give Gilbert a voice. He feels closer affinities with the Batswana and is more readily accepted by them.

Dinorego is another misfit. He is the only man in the village who is a full-time crop grower. Batswana men traditionally spurned this activity in favor of animal husbandry and hunting. What strikes Makhaya on first seeing Dinorego is the disparity between his tattered clothes and his serene aura. This unusual and unpretentious sage remarks: " 'In this world are born both evil and good men. Both have to do justice to their cause. In this country there is a great tolerance of evil. It is because of death that we tolerate evil. All meet death in the end, and because of death we make allowance for evil though we do not like it' " (*Rain Clouds,* 27). This statement anticipates the concerted action of the villagers in their spirited stand against Matenge. Combined with this passivity in the face of evil is the innate progressiveness that Dinorego identifies in the Batswana: " 'A Batswana man thinks like this: "If there is a way to improve my life, I shall do it." . . . Each time he feels he has improved himself a little, he is ready to try a new idea' " (25).

It is to this spirit of cautious progressiveness in the villagers of Golema Mmidi that Gilbert appeals. With Makhaya as his right-hand man he hopes to transform the face of suffering in the village. In this quest he gives fictional expression to Head's often-articulated desire for leaders who are at once practical and idealistic, who eschew high political office for grassroots activity. In an interview in 1983 she remarked: "Poverty has been with me all my life, but [in Botswana] it was like a shared social problem. . . . [T]he poverty of people demands an immediate kind of solution. The scale on which I worked was not like a huge religious propaganda" (*Between the Lines,* 9).

Head modeled the character of Makhaya on a young Zimbabwean refugee she met in Francistown in 1967. She describes the meeting in this way: "A young refugee from Zimbabwe quietly detached himself from the group and held long dialogues with me. He didn't want to go for military training. He had no faith in the future black leadership of Zimbabwe because there was no one articulating the hopes of the people and he did not want to die for a worthless cause" (*Woman Alone,* 73). Her skepticism about the integrity of many black nationalist leaders she pours into the character Joas Tsepe, whom she portrays as brash, opportunistic, and ignorant. Tsepe represents the "fashionable political ideologies of the new Africa" (*Rain Clouds,* 45), movements that were spawned in the wake of colonialism. The preferred vehicle for change proposed in the novel is "the natural growth of a people" (*Rain Clouds,* 45). This Head perceives to be germane to the Botswana national character, making the country a special case in postcolonial Africa. A typically wry description of Botswana's uniqueness in this regard appears in a discursive passage: "The tide of African nationalism had swept down the con-

tinent and then faltered at the northern borders of Botswana. During
the pre-election campaign, the politicians had had to chase after the
people who kept on moving back and forth to their cattle posts and
lands, seemingly unaware that destiny was about to catch up with
them" (*Rain Clouds,* 62).

In *Rain Clouds,* political ideology is presented as an imposition on the
natural development of the Batswana people. Pan-Africanism in particular is singled out for criticism: "To many, Pan-Africanism is an almost
sacred dream, but like all dreams it also has its nightmare side, and the
little men like Joas Tsepe and their strange doings are the nightmare. If
they have any power at all it is the power to plunge the African continent into an era of chaos and bloody murder" (47). Not only are the
Pan-Africanists political opportunists but their backing is sinister. Tsepe,
we are told, is supported by "some mysterious source" that pays all his
expenses, including the purchase of a motor car (47). At one point in the
novel the following question is asked: "Was it perhaps the intention of
the secret financier to re-establish the rule of the illiterate and semiliterate man in Africa?" (48).

Head's clear preference is for the kind of evolutionary growth exemplified in the activities of cooperatives in the economic sphere and mod-
erate, pragmatic government in the political sphere. In this sort of government people like Paramount Chief Sekoto, Matenge's senior brother,
and George Appleby-Smith, the local colonial administrator, are exemplary lower-level representatives. Sekoto is opposed to tribalism in its
most narrow and insidious form, despite the benefits he accrues by
virtue of his position in the system. Appleby-Smith represents a curious
mixture of officious authoritarianism and humane realism. Together the
men serve as facilitators for the more active agents of change in the form
of Gilbert and Makhaya.

Matenge's response to Makhaya, by contrast, is simpleminded and
vindictive. In this he echoes the sentiments of the South African government. " 'Either I go or the refugee goes,' " he declaims to his brother. "
'How can people feel safe with a criminal and murderer in their midst?
That is what the story says; he is a criminal and murderer who walks
around with bombs in his pocket. Why should Gilbert take in such a
man unless it is his intention to murder me?' " (*Rain Clouds,* 54).

There are a number of elements at work in this passage. First there is
the irony about people not feeling safe. Matenge is the greatest threat to
their security. Then there is the idiotic distortion of the details about
Makhaya's arrest by the South African government. He was arrested

and detained for carrying plans for sabotage. He did not have actual bombs in his pocket, nor is it physically possible for anyone simply to carry bombs in his trouser pocket. The main point, however, is that the South African government and subchief Matenge are clearly the two faces of the same kind of oppression. Head sees this unholy alliance between African tribalism and neocolonial oppression as the real threat to progress through evolutionary change in southern Africa.

The form that evolutionary change will take is uncertain in *When Rain Clouds Gather*. Consider the following sentiment voiced by Gilbert: " 'Golema Mmidi has the exact amount of rainfall of a certain area in southern Africa where Turkish tobacco is grown very successfully. It's a very good cash crop too, and if everyone in Golema Mmidi grows a bit and we market it co-operatively—why, we'll all be rich in no time' " (*Rain Clouds*, 59). Getting rich quickly smacks of the opportunism of the new breed of African politicians and, indeed, of their colonial masters before them. Is Head, through Gilbert, expressing a belief in the liberatory potential of capitalistic market principles? Does she believe that the accumulation of capital through profitable marketing will raise the standard of living in Golema Mmidi and, ultimately, that of Botswana as a whole?

Head's support for capitalist development, at odds with the socialist spirit of the cooperatives she professes also to support, is evident in this passage and runs as a theme throughout the novel. Simon Simonse argues this point in his discussion of the novel: "We might as well be frank about it from the start: Bessie Head does believe in the emancipatory potential of capitalist development. It is her contention that small-scale capitalism on a co-operative basis offers a realistic opportunity for revolutionizing the stagnated relations of production in the countryside. *When Rain Clouds Gather* describes such a revolution."[2]

That the novel asserts the necessity of "small-scale capitalism on a co-operative basis" is undeniable. This does not necessarily constitute an endorsement of a process that will lead to exploitive social and economic relations, however. It is essential that the Batswana develop and utilize their natural resources, yet this development is to be guarded closely by the proviso that all benefits accrue to the people themselves. Cooperative development, or communalism, is therefore the antithesis of rampant capitalism in *When Rain Clouds Gather*.

The precise nature of this development and path to general prosperity nevertheless remains problematic in the novel. Because Head does not conform to a recognized program of political activity, her view of economic development is largely undefined. The key to this indetermi-nacy lies in her conceptual orientation: she does not work from a pre-conceived political ideology and apply it to the issue at hand. With Bessie Head, abstract moral principles have much more weight and are by their very nature less easily translated into political and social prac-tice. For her, generosity, courtesy, and respect for the common person are the touchstones to positive social, political, and economic strategies. This orientation, however, is not without its own difficulties. Arthur Ravenscroft expresses his reservations about the novel in the following way: "The precise relationship between individual freedom and political independence, and between a guarded core of privacy and an unbudding towards others, may seem rather elusive, perhaps even mystical . . . and I see it as one of the weaknesses of *When Rain Clouds Gather*."[3]

Makhaya Maseko's quest in the novel is to find inner peace by a con-structive engagement with the social world. In the ideal world of Golema Mmidi both of these desires are offered fulfillment. His involve-ment in cooperative farming is matched by cooperation at an emotional human level. In Golema Mmidi he finds people willing to share their goods, both material and spiritual. The "feeling of great goodness" that permeates the life of the village translates into both practical activity and human cooperation (*Rain Clouds,* 184).

This "feeling of goodness" is crucial to the success of the fictive world Head creates in *Rain Clouds.* It is the unexamined "given" from which she is able to construct a tenuous link between the public and the pri-vate. The weakness of this link is revealed in the attitudes Paulina and Mma-Millipede have toward the cooperatives. They do not enter the project with an awareness of what it stands for, what it means to the economic life of the subsistence dwellers of Golema Mmidi. Their moti-vations are personal. When Gilbert anxiously asks Mma-Millipede to recommend a woman who will start cooperative tobacco farming under Makhaya's supervision, she sees this as an opportunity to match Paulina with Makhaya. The link between the personal and the social thus becomes fortuitous, indeterminate.

This is an example of the whole tone of the novel: everything positive develops by happy accident. The introduction of the "God with no shoes" (*Rain Clouds,* 185) at the end of the novel is an attempt to make events less arbitrary—to compensate for the absence of a causal connec-tion between them. This is why the novel has been accused of being excessively romantic (Ravenscroft, 179). The romantic element is reflected in the novel's traditional happy ending. Matters come to a head when Matenge summons Paulina to his house to punish her for her role in spearheading female involvement in the new agricultural project Gilbert and Makhaya have organized. Matenge misjudges the will of the people, who gather outside his house to demand an explanation for his actions. The combined force of the villagers, led by Gilbert, Makhaya, and Paulina drives the subchief to suicide. Cooperative farming is at least tentatively established, and both Gilbert and Makhaya put the seal on their commitment to Botswana by marrying Batswana women.

Another conceptual problem in the novel arises in Head's portrayal of political process. For her, both white neocolonial oppression and black nationalist backlash impede the progress of Africa as a whole. With the "hate-making political ideologies" of newly independent Africa come a new set of reactionary ideas. They provoke a mania and paranoia in the person that embraces them, the novel argues, and the exponents of these ideologies are considered "pompous, bombastic fools" (*Rain Clouds*, 80). For Head, the way out of this vicious binary opposition is to strike out on a personal course.

Makhaya is not swayed by popular political movements. He is both of the people and yet apart. He comes increasingly to assert his separateness and amid mass confusion turns more and more to his inner resources as a guide. This stance is unusual in Africa:

> It was an uphill task in a part of the world where everyone tended to cling to his or her precious prejudice and tradition, and the act of letting go of it all greatly increased a man's foes. You find yourself throwing blows but weeping at the same time, because of all the people who sit and wail in the darkness, and because of all the fat smug persecutors to whom this wailing is like sweet music, and some inner voice keeps on telling you that your way is right for you, that the process of rising up from the darkness is an intensely personal and private one, and that if you can find a society that leaves the individual to develop freely you ought to choose that society as your home. (*Rain Clouds*, 80)

In *When Rain Clouds Gather* (as in *Maru*, as we shall see), the "inner voice" is the source of truth. Individuals plot separate, personal courses through life; they achieve personal goals and destinies. This is the way out of the darkness and confusion in which the African continent is plunged. As I have already shown, this conception is poorly integrated into the avowedly socialist orientation the novel argues for in the socioeconomic sphere.

Head herself was aware of the flaws in her first novel, which she later described as "my most amateur effort" (*Woman Alone,* 64). That she came to be embarrassed by its amateurishness and naive idealism is also evident in another remark she made: "The central character in the novel, a black South African refugee, is almost insipid, a guileless, simple-hearted simpleton" (68). That she later turned so vehemently on her hero is somewhat surprising; after all, she was sufficiently impressed by the young refugee on whom she modeled Makhaya to structure the novel around his activities.

An explanation for this volte-face can be sought in Head's greater wisdom in her later years. Makhaya undoubtedly exhibits some of the impulsiveness and naivete she herself possessed when she wrote *Rain Clouds.* James Matthews made the following remark about the youthful Head: "Politically naive on her arrival in Cape Town, she drank in political ideologies. The experience left her with a hangover resulting in a distrust of all political systems" (Matthews, 9). This remark also explains Head's ignorance of politics, which resulted in the reductive polarities in *Rain Clouds* between the "evil tribalists" on the one hand and the "peace-loving and progressive villagers" on the other.

Another weak aspect of the novel is characterization. The various characters tend to play preordained, unidimensional roles and often fail to take on a life of their own. The "evil" characters particularly are flat and unconvincing: no compelling explanation is given for their vendetta against Gilbert and Makhaya, and they remain mere engines of hate, ill-defined vessels into which the author can pour her own unresolved fears and uncertainties.

For all its weaknesses, however, *When Rain Clouds Gather* is a bold and courageous first work by a writer working in very strained circumstances. The novel shows some of the innovative qualities that characterize Head's later work and that set her writing off from other more conventional African novelists. The theme of conflict between old and new, for instance—a recurring theme in African fiction since Achebe's *Things Fall Apart* (1958)—is given a fresh direction in *Rain Clouds.* Head inverts the customary story line of this genre (which generally focuses on the protagonist's passage from his rural village to the bright lights of the city, with all of its opportunities and pitfalls) and eschews a simplistic paradigm of racial conflict in southern Africa by constructing the possibility of interracial cooperation and friendship.

Head's attempt to resolve her protagonist's inner struggle in *Rain Clouds* by constructing an ideal world in which his innermost needs are met is ultimately unsatisfactory (as the previous discussion has suggested), and this is why she takes up the same themes again with greater urgency in *Maru*. The moral and existential complexity of Head's vision does not allow for a facile resolution, and thus the novel ends on a deeply ambivalent note. At the novel's conclusion, Makhaya feels "as though everything was uncertain, new and strange and beginning from scratch" (*Rain Clouds*, 188).

Chapter Five
Maru (1971)

Maru, which derives its name from its central male character, is an altogether more complex work than its predecessor. It is a story about a young girl who is sent to an outlying Botswanan village as a teacher. She is a *Masarwa,* a word the Tswana use to denote people of the Bushman or San race. The word is defined in the novel as the Tswana "equivalent of 'nigger,' a term of contempt which means, obliquely, a low, filthy nation."[1] The girl is Margaret Cadmore, named after her adoptive mother, the wife of a missionary from England. Margaret Cadmore adopts the girl after her mother dies in childbirth on the outskirts of the village. The local people are reluctant to bury the dead woman, so they call in the missionaries, who "had been known to go into queer places because of their occupation" (*Maru,* 12). Margaret Cadmore senior is described as having common sense "in over-abundance," even if she lacks the rarer quality of "love of mankind" (12–13). She observes astutely that the Masarwa people " 'don't seem to be at all a part of the life of this country' " and is determined to change this (13). Armed with her notion of "environment everything; heredity nothing," she brings up her young charge as an "experiment" to prove this theory (15).

As a result of the unusual circumstances of her birth, the young Margaret Cadmore grows up with "a big hole" in her mind (*Maru,* 15), a space that is usually taken up with an awareness of background, home environment, and family ancestry. She is "hardly African or anything but something new and universal, a type of personality that would be unable to fit into a definition of something as narrow as tribe or race or nation" (16). As a "real, living object for her experiment," she is equipped by her mother with "good sense and logical arguments," which "mean in the end that almost anything could be thrown into her mind and life and she would have the capacity, within herself, to survive both heaven and hell" (15, 16).

Heaven and hell is what she encounters in Dilepe village, where she is sent as a newly qualified teacher by the missionary woman, who tells her that " 'one day, you will help your people' " (*Maru,* 17). On arrival Margaret first meets Dikeledi, an attractive and forthright woman who becomes a valuable ally in Margaret's struggle to negotiate the powerful undercurrents of village life. With characteristic honesty, Margaret responds to Dikeledi's query about her origins with the bland statement " 'I am a Masarwa' " (24). Dikeledi's response is a portent of the abuse that is to come: "Dikeledi drew in her breath with a sharp, hissing sound. Dilepe village was the stronghold of some of the most powerful and wealthy chiefs in the country, all of whom owned innumerable Masarwa as slaves" (24). A little later we discover that "it wasn't for her own sake . . . that she drew in a sharp, hissing breath"; rather, it was "an instinctive, protective gesture" toward Margaret (25).

Dikeledi is the daughter of a paramount chief and the sister of Maru, who will soon succeed his father as chief of the tribe. Margaret next meets Moleka, with whom Dikeledi is hopelessly in love despite his appearance when we first meet him as "grim and vehement and gruesomely ugly" (*Maru,* 27). After rebuffing Margaret and Dikeledi, who approach him in the Dilepe Tribal Administration offices with a request for accommodation for Margaret, he then shows his other "smiling" face and offers Margaret accommodation in a vacant old library and supplies her with a bed. On arrival there, Margaret becomes aware of his disconcertingly changeable nature: "A moment ago he had been a hateful, arrogant man. Now, he had another face which made him seem the most beautiful person on earth" (29–30). Margaret is immediately attracted to him and feels her loneliness disappearing "like the mist before the warmth of a rising sun" (30). She looks out over the village below, which appears to her to be suffused with a warm, romantic glow: "A thousand wisps of blue smoke arose silently into the air as a thousand women prepared the evening meal beside their outdoor fires. That peace, and those darkening evening shadows were to be the rhythm of her life throughout that year, and Dilepe village was to seem the most beautiful village on earth" (31).

For his part, Moleka feels as if "something had gone 'bang!' inside his chest," a sensation "not like anything he had felt before" (*Maru,* 32). Dikeledi, he reflects, "made his bloodstream boil," but this was something different: "It was like finding inside himself a gold mine he'd not known was there before." He is puzzled by the uncustomary feeling Margaret has awakened in him and feels that "some other person had prepared him for his encounter with the woman" (32). In this way we are introduced to Moleka's "shadow," Maru. Maru and Moleka "lived in each other's arms and shared everything. . . . [N]o experiences interrupted the river and permanent flow of their deep affection" (33). As a sign of what is to come, however, we read that Moleka, so "involved in this river . . . never had time to notice the strange and unpredictable evolution of his friend." This is the first suggestion of the conflict that is to come when Maru also falls in love with Margaret.

Maru is portrayed as having greater spiritual depth than Moleka. In his "kingdom" he is able to "mix the prosaic of everyday life with the sudden beauty of a shooting star" (*Maru*, 34). Like Moleka, he indulges in short-lived affairs with young women in the village, "but it never went far because it always turned out that Miss so-and-so had no kingdom of her own" (34). In his search for a partner with a "kingdom" of her own it is inevitable that Maru will come across Margaret. Up to this point he has encountered only women "who confused the inner Maru, who was a king of heaven, with the outer Maru and his earthly position of future paramount chief of a tribe" (35). When his relationship with one of these women fell through, "the girl would flee the village or become insane." As a result, a "terror slowly built up around the name of Maru," and the people begin speculating that he was "the reincarnation of Tladi, a monstrous ancestral African witch-doctor who had been a performer of horrific magic" (36). Only Moleka knows all the secrets of Maru's heart, however, and "since no other came so close to the heart of Maru, they invented all kinds of rubbish and horrors" (37). Moleka believes that this closeness between them will be eternal, but Maru, with his superior insight and prescience, knows that it will last only until they both fall in love with the same woman.

Margaret's equilibrium is disturbed at the start of the new school term by her encounter with Pete, the school's principal. Described as being "a little like Uriah Heep, and a belly-crawler to anyone he considered more important than himself" (*Maru*, 39), Pete discovers to his shock that his new staff member is not a "Coloured," as he first thought, but a "Masarwa." He is soon involved in an intrigue with Seth, the education supervisor of the area, to get rid of this embarrassment. Seth advises caution, however, and says that he will seek the opinion of the "Totems," the tribal aristocrats who have been running tribal affairs since the death of the old paramount chief some months before. Revealingly, the two men cannot believe that the woman Margaret could have got the job on her own merits, and they assume that someone higher up was "pushing her" (41). The Totems themselves are uneasy with the current state of tribal affairs: Maru, the paramount chief-elect, is to be installed sometime during the year, and they are not yet sure which side he will take. Seth and Pete have set their hopes on sidelining Maru and installing his younger brother, Morafi, who is more to their liking: "Like most Totems, Morafi was a cattle thief and he had had a hey-day of thieving while his father was alive, his father being a thief as well" (42). The future course that the tribe will take hangs in the balance: will Maru, upon attaining power, fall in with tradition and become another in a long line of self-aggrandizers, or will he lead the society in a completely new direction?

Only two Totems, Dikeledi and Moleka, exclude themselves from the intrigue that now envelops the village, but they perform actions that prove momentous: "The action of one crippled Pete, the action of the other caused a wave of shame to sweep through the hearts of ordinary people" (*Maru*, 45). Pete incites a schoolboy to lead an insurrection against the new teacher. The next day in the classroom the boy, looking into Margaret's face with an "insolent stare," asks: " 'Since when is a Bushy a teacher?' " (45). The ensuing uproar, in which the children chant " 'You are a Bushman,' " is the cue for Pete to step in and dismiss the teacher on the grounds that she is not able to control her class. Dikeledi intervenes before he can do this, however, and restores order by forcing the children to recognize Margaret's status as their teacher. Pete's plan backfires, and all of the teachers take advantage of the turn of events to laugh openly at his cowardly and conniving behavior.

Moleka does something even more disturbing to the conservative villagers: in a dramatic symbolic gesture he invites his Masarwa slaves to eat with him at his table and ensures that Seth is there to witness the occasion. The whole village is thrown into upheaval: "Something they liked as Africans to pretend themselves incapable of was being exposed to oppression and prejudice. They always knew it was there but no oppressor believes in his oppression. He always says he treats his slaves nicely. He never says that there ought not to be slaves" (*Maru*, 48).

When Maru returns from a visit to some remote villages he is apprised of the dramatic events by Ranko, one of his "spies." On learning that Moleka has fallen in love with Margaret (which prompted his bold gesture of eating with his Masarwa slaves), Maru lays plans to unseat him and to rid the village of Seth, Morafi, and Pete. He confronts Moleka at the administration offices and is astonished at the transformation in the man: "The savage, arrogant Moleka was no longer there, but some other person like himself—humbled and defeated before all the beauty of the living world" (*Maru*, 57). He is momentarily unsettled but then looks deeper into Moleka's apparent transformation: "The humility was superficial, perhaps in keeping with his changed view of himself, but what was in Moleka's heart, now that the barriers were broken, made Maru's heart cold with fear. It was another version of arrogance and dominance, but more terrible because it was of the spirit" (57–58). Maru sees Moleka's newly unleashed power as "a sun around which spun a billion satellites," whereas his own kingdom "had no sun like that, only an eternal and gentle interplay of shadows and peace" (58). Moleka has an "over-abundance of power," whereas he has "creative imagination . . . in over-abundance."

Moleka, Maru concludes (either disinterestedly or out of jealousy), is not worthy of Margaret's love, and Moleka's recent act of liberating his slaves would not achieve the desired effect: "Why, any wild horse was also powerful and where did wild horses go? They jumped over cliffs. Moleka and his stupid brain would send all those billion worlds colliding into each other" (*Maru,* 58). Maru then sets his plan in motion. Assuming the demeanor of a die-hard traditionalist, he forces Moleka to revoke the loan of the bed to Margaret. The action has the desired effect: Margaret's equilibrium is "shattered" (61). She comes down to the offices to speak to Moleka and is confronted by Maru, who reiterates the demand to return the bed, saying that it is his wish that she do so. Margaret can only accede to his demand and walk out "as if she were facing her death" (64). On her departure Maru muses to himself, and a "picture slowly unfolded itself before him": "How often had it haunted his mind. There was a busy, roaring highway on one side, full of bustle and traffic. Leading away from it was a small, dusty footpath. It went on and on by itself into the distance. 'Take that path,' his heart said. 'You have no other choice' " (64). This is the first indication that Maru will choose not to accede to power but to retreat to his rural haven and leave political power in the hands of others. Significantly, it is his first glimpse of Margaret that prompts this vision: he now senses that he may have a companion to accompany him on the "small, dusty footpath."

When he tells his sister Dikeledi that he has forced Margaret to return the bed, she responds with shock and disbelief. His cool rejoinder throws her into still further confusion: " 'I don't care whether she sleeps on the hard floor for the rest of her life but I am not going to marry a pampered doll' " (*Maru,* 66). Her response—" 'But you can't marry a Masarwa. Not in your position' "—shows up both the superficiality of her defense of Margaret as a full human being and also the comprehensiveness of the social reform Maru is envisaging. He envisions a "world apart from petty human hatreds and petty human social codes and values where the human soul roamed free in all its splendour and glory"

(67), and his marrying a member of an outcast, despised race group will effect the transformation of the present society into this new one. His role, however, will be one largely of making symbolic gestures. " 'I was not born to rule this mess,' " he tells Dikeledi. " 'If I have a place it is to pull down the old structures and create the new' " (68). He is capable of projecting the kind of "creative ferment" that could change the society, but he is not a "living dynamo" that could institute this change in practical ways (70). Dikeledi and Moleka are equipped for this role, he believes: "Moleka and Dikeledi were the future kings and queens of the African continent, those of stature and goodness. He, Maru, was the dreamer of this future greatness" (70).

Maru sets his plans in motion. He sends Ranko to convey a message to the lovesick Moleka: " 'Tell Moleka to remember that he enjoys life on this earth. This is not the end for him. He will have a long life' " (*Maru*, 78). Moleka initially responds with anger at this clear instruction to leave Margaret alone but then falls in with Maru's plans by reestablishing his relationship with Dikeledi: "Dikeledi's kingdom was like that of the earth and its deep centre which absorbed the light and radiations of a billion suns and planets" (83).

Dikeledi, for her part, becomes Maru's unwitting agent. She discovers that Margaret, like her missionary mother, is an artist. Margaret Cadmore junior, however, is the superior artist: "The older Margaret Cadmore had been essentially a cold and unemotional woman, insensitive to the depths and heights of life, and the young girl high-lighted these latter qualities, at the same time emulating her skill for rapid reproduction of life" (87). The pictures that Margaret paints later become the means by which Maru is able to gauge her spiritual depth and also track her inexorable progress toward convergence with his own destiny.

In the meantime, the Pete, Seth, and Morafi trio has to be removed. Maru sets his two other spies, Moseka and Semana, on their trail. The pair haunt and tantalize their victims to the point where they eventually flee the village in disarray: "No coherent explanations were ever given, except that the people who lived with them all thought they had suddenly lost their minds" (*Maru*, 92). So once again, by scheming and manipulating, Maru is able to turn events in his favor. By the end of part 1 of the novel, Moleka has been redirected from his infatuation with Margaret to his original love for Dikeledi, Dikeledi herself has been unwittingly installed as Maru's agent, and Pete, Seth, and Morafi have been eliminated.

   The short second part of the novel focuses principally on Maru's plans
for Margaret. The latter is still blissfully in love with Moleka and
unaware of the plans being hatched. Dikeledi supplies her with painting
materials and urges her to spend the school holidays painting while she
herself attends a conference in another village. Margaret launches herself
into days of nonstop activity: "Life was totally disrupted and another
rhythm replaced it which made day and night merge into a restless
fever. . . . There was a part of her mind that had saturated itself with
things of such startling beauty and they pressed, in determined
panorama, to take on living form" (*Maru*, 100–101).
   On her return Dikeledi surveys the achievements of the past days and
separates three pictures from the others: they all have a common theme,
"a pulsating glow of yellow light dominating pitch black objects"
(*Maru*, 102). Margaret herself is not entirely able to explain these pictures: " 'I had a strange experience,' she said slowly. 'Each time I closed
my eyes those pictures used to fill all the space inside my head' " (103).
She goes on to relate how she had visions of a house, a footpath sur-
rounded by yellow daisies, and a couple embracing. To her surprise,
Dikeledi sees that the man depicted in one of the three paintings closely
resembles Maru. "How had he done it?" she muses. "How had he projected his dreams on someone so far removed from him?" (104). Maru's
response when he receives the paintings from Dikeledi is characteristically self-assured: " 'I was waiting for them,' he said quietly" (105).
Later he remarks to himself: " 'If we have the same dreams, perhaps that
means something' " (107).
   Shortly before Maru's final plans for Margaret are set in motion,
Dikeledi mysteriously tells her: " 'You will be surprised at whom you
will marry one day' " (*Maru*, 114). Margaret is still helplessly in love
with Moleka, unaware that her friend has set her own heart on him and
unaware also that Maru is the person to whom Dikeledi had cryptically
referred. The moment is a quiet prelude to the storm that is to follow:
"She was to remember those words one day when certain events
occurred to throw her from the quiet, static niche she had found for herself" (114). In her last painting, Margaret records "the hour of peace"
preceding the events that cause her "to become another Dikeledi who
alternated happiness with misery, finding herself tossed about this way
and that on permanently restless seas" (115). Significantly, Maru refuses
to accept this last painting when Dikeledi presents it to him, saying
simply: " 'It's not for me' " (116). He knows that it is meant for Moleka,

who later lavishes "adoration and attention" on it, realizing that it is Margaret's abiding testament of her love for him.

The first dramatic event to occur is Dikeledi's sudden announcement that she is pregnant and is soon to marry Moleka. The effect of this news on Margaret is devastating: "A few vital threads of her life had snapped behind her neck and it felt as though she were shrivelling to death" (*Maru,* 118). Maru's response on hearing how badly she has taken the news is cool: " 'Let her suffer a bit. It will teach her to appreciate other things' " (120). The wedding takes place amid great revelry, but Dikeledi is upset at the visible enmity between Moleka and Maru. For his part, Moleka is angry at what is now clear to him—that Maru had "forcefully engineered the marriage" (120)—and he is determined to prevent Maru from taking Margaret as his lover.

Maru outmaneuvers him, however, by going in secret to Margaret with his aides, Ranko, Semana, and Moseka, and arranging to remove her from the village. Still stunned by the recent turn of events, she succumbs to Maru's gentle persuasiveness: " 'We used to dream the same dreams. That was how I knew you would love me in the end,' " he says to her (*Maru,* 124). Her feelings contain the fundamental ambiguities that are henceforth to characterize her life with Maru: "What could she say, except that at that moment she would have chosen anything as an alternative to the living death into which she had so unexpectedly fallen" (124). They leave the village together, "heading straight for a home, a thousand miles away where the sun rose, new and new and new each day" (125).

Moleka's response on hearing the news is rueful: " 'So he has fooled me once again. I knew I'd never get her from him. He's the devil!' " (*Maru,* 125). He settles down to married life with Dikeledi with greater equanimity, however, the dispute between him and Maru now finally put to rest. The response of the villagers is less forgiving: "When people of Dilepe village heard about the marriage of Maru, they began to talk about him as if he had died. . . . They knew nothing about the standards of the soul, and since Maru only lived by those standards they had never been able to make a place for him in their society" (126). For the Masarwa people, when Maru married Margaret "a door silently opened on the small, dark airless room in which their souls had been shut for a long time" (126). The novel ends on a triumphal note: "People like the Batswana, who did not know that the wind of freedom had also reached people of the Masarwa tribe, were in for an unpleasant surprise because it would be no longer possible to treat Masarwa people in an inhuman way without getting killed yourself" (127).

One is immediately aware, when reading *Maru*, that *Maru* and *Rain Clouds* belong to different orders of fiction. *Maru* has different rules for its internal coherence and also for its interpretation by the reader. A striking example of this is that the novel opens with an epilogue to the events that unfold through the rest of the novel. So chronology is disrupted and the reader is apprised of the outcome of the novel's events at the outset. Arthur Ravenscroft calls this device "a species of sealed orders for the reader" (Ravenscroft, 179). The linear progression of events in *Rain Clouds* is thus replaced by the circular pattern of *Maru*, and our understanding of events throughout the novel is fashioned by our prior knowledge of their eventual outcome. The last pages of the novel invite us to return to the beginning to reread the opening pages with an enlarged understanding. The element of surprise, the desire to learn the outcome of events, is no longer the driving force behind the narrative. The invitation is to read more deeply into already known events, to dwell more seriously on the wider social and metaphysical significance of the human drama.

The rivalry of Maru and Moleka is that of two powerful personalities vying for supremacy. Maru is portrayed as being manipulative and perceptive, Moleka as bright, passionate, and energetic. Through most of the story it is Maru who has the upper hand; he has "creative imagination," whereas Moleka has energy without the imagination to direct it: "They were kings of opposing kingdoms. It was Moleka's kingdom that was unfathomable, as though shut behind a heavy iron door. There had been no such door for Maru. He dwelt everywhere" (*Maru*, 58, 34).

Maru's godlike omniscience gives him ascendancy, but this is threatened by the love Margaret awakens in Moleka. Moleka's power is latent: it is an unknown quantity that Maru fears. With the awakening of his love for Margaret, Moleka's energy becomes channeled: he feels an indefinable surge of power. Maru's calculations are momentarily unbalanced, but he deftly averts this threat to his supremacy by engineering first the marriage of Moleka to his sister and ultimately his own marriage to Margaret. He abdicates political responsibility and moves away from Dilepe village, leaving tribal authority in the hands of Moleka. The social implications of Maru's marriage are profound: Margaret comes from a race of untouchables.

Some years after the publication of *Maru,* Head made the following comment about the Masarwa: "Basarwa people were . . . abhorrent to Botswana people because they hardly looked African, but Chinese. I knew the language of racial hatred but it was an evil exclusively practised by white people. I therefore listened in amazement as Botswana people talked of the Basarwa whom they oppressed: 'They don't think,' they said. 'They don't know anything' " (*Woman Alone,* 69). Head's avowed purpose in writing *Maru* was "to write an enduring novel on the hideousness of racial prejudice" (68). The novel's exploration of the personal dramas springing from a love triangle can therefore be seen to have wider implications for Botswanan society in general. They become a critique of race prejudice and narrow, reactionary tribal custom. That Maru, a paramount chief-elect, could marry a Masarwa, an untouchable slave, jars the complacency of the Batswana and opens the door of change to the Masarwa. However, as with *Rain Clouds,* the link between personal drama and social resonance is not satisfactorily demonstrated. This weakness is part of a greater problem in Head's social understanding, to which I shall return later.

Having recognized the complexity of the emotions of those acting out the human drama, and also the social implications of this drama, one nevertheless senses that a more profound level of meaning lies beneath the novel's surface realism. A single passage describing Maru demonstrates this: "There had never been a time in his life when he had not thought a thought and felt it immediately bound to the deep centre of the earth, then bound back to his heart again—with a reply" (*Maru,* 7). It is clear when reading *Maru* that individual characters are meant to stand for something else, that individual actions and events are a way of expressing things that go beyond the confines of narrative realism. Two realms of significance are deeply buried in the text: the deepest interior workings of the human psyche and the creative activity of the artist. These run as subtexts beneath the novel's surface.

One of the principles of the realist novel is that its narrative pattern should be complete in itself. Symbolism and noncausal cross-reference are secondary to the narrative pattern and should never assume primacy. Clearly, the story line of *Maru,* the sequence of concrete daily events, is simply a point of departure for Head: it is there to serve the needs of higher levels of meaning. It follows that the logic of this pattern of events is not one of externally observable cause and effect. What gives coherence to events in *Maru* are the inner workings of the minds of the characters. The drama becomes internal; the subjects enter into relationships with each other at a psychic level.

The psychic plane—or in Head's terms, the realm of the soul—is accessible only to Maru, Moleka, and Margaret. The novel therefore becomes a three-sided struggle in the realm of the soul. Each of these characters has dual identities, one applying to the real world and the other a "soul-identity." In Maru's case there is the "inner Maru," who is a "king of heaven" (*Maru*, 35), and the outer Maru, who is the future paramount chief of his tribe. The inner Maru is the superbeing who is in union with the inexorable workings of the universe; he is part of the cosmic whole.

The dynamic of alienation and commitment at work in Head's first three novels is given a fresh direction in *Maru*. The characters' movement from alienation to commitment (a physical journey in the realism of *Rain Clouds*) is a journey of the soul in *Maru*. Maru's quest is to attain the realm of the inner self, the being in touch with the secret pulse of the universe. He moves from the alienation of his tribal, exterior identity to his inner identity as a "king of heaven" (*Maru*, 35). Similarly, Margaret's journey from alienation to wholeness is a passage from her racially ascribed identity to her true inner identity. (Head's contention is that socially ascribed identities are false, misleading, degrading to the true inner person.) Through the union of two equal souls, Maru and Margaret defy the prejudiced world and point to a new world of true racial equality.

The second subtext that runs through the novel is a commentary on the nature of art and of the artist. Margaret Cadmore senior was in the habit of sketching people and events in the village. She did this partly to control her frustration with people, whom she generally regarded as inordinately stupid. Her art is therefore therapeutic: she releases her impatience with the rest of humankind by sketching people and then writing satirical captions for the sketches. This creates a distance between her and her subjects. In the process, she becomes an aloof, skeptical recorder of human folly: "Margaret Cadmore was not the kind of woman to speculate on how any artistic observation of human suffering arouses infinite compassion" (*Maru*, 14).

When she comes across the dying Bushman woman (the heroine's mother), she discovers that her art is limited: something about the Bushman woman arrests her artistic impulse. Here she is presented with life that is too close to the bone for her satirical perspective. Her kind of art cannot do justice to this subject. Yet she creates a person (Margaret, her adopted daughter) whose art and humanity are all-powerful and all-embracing. From an early age Margaret has "a vantage point from which she could observe the behaviour of a persecutor" (*Maru*, 17). She has the true artist's grasp of the whole of humanity and the ability to penetrate to the heart of things, to understand the deepest motives in people. Like Head herself, Margaret turns inward as a defense against a hostile society. Her alienation from the Batswana and her isolation from her own people make her a kind of internal exile. This, however, allows her to transcend race, national, and class boundaries: "She was a little bit of everything in the whole universe, because the woman who had educated her was the universe itself" (20).

Maru has mastery over this universe, and Margaret gains access to this realm through her art. She is therefore his ideal partner. As we saw, after encountering her art Maru muses to himself: " 'If we have the same dreams, perhaps that means something' " (*Maru*, 107). Cherry Wilhelm describes this correspondence in the following way: "The 'proof' of artistic authenticity is that her images flow from that level of unconscious underlife where Maru's dreams meet hers."[2] The two undercurrents in the novel—the exploration of the realm of the soul and the activity of the artist—meet at this point.

Head is concerned with opposing a trend in her society that she considers destructive and debasing: racism, prejudice, and avarice. In the figure of Maru—who "set the tone . . . for a new world" (*Maru*, 50)—she creates an opponent of these pernicious trends. Head is not able to resolve with satisfaction the problem of reconciling personal fulfillment with public commitment, however. Her ideal is the fulfillment of individual desires, but her context is one in which there are huge economic and social problems that require urgent attention. This creates a structural tension in her work, a tension she attempts to resolve in *Maru* by splitting a character in two, each part of which fulfills a different yet equally necessary role: Maru points the way to the future, and Moleka acts it out.

The consequence of this is that a host of problems attend on the novel's ending. Margaret and Dikeledi are permanent casualties of Maru's maneuverings: as we saw, Margaret "was to become another Dikeledi who alternated happiness with misery, finding herself tossed about this way and that on permanently restless seas" (*Maru*, 115). Maru's treatment of Margaret is highly questionable. At one point he tells Dikeledi to inform him immediately if anyone else shows an interest in Margaret so that he can "mess everything up" (72). Even more alarming, when toward the conclusion of the novel he has self-doubts and asks himself what he will do if she does not love him as much as he loves her, the "terrible reply" that "came from his heart" is " 'Kill her' " (111). Lastly, that she should be regarded as a sovereign individual with her own volition is brutally negated in Maru's final act of taking her away, an act that amounts to nothing less than abduction.

If one takes seriously Head's claim to write "didactic" novels (*Woman Alone,* 62), it is clear that what she is preaching against in *Maru* is racial prejudice. Her moral condemnation of this iniquity is unequivocal. What is not clear is the alternative that is projected. *Maru* is offered on one level as a way to end racial antagonism: there is a real sense that Head is concerned with engaging with the real world, instituting change, putting an end to prejudice and reactionary codes of behavior, and establishing genuine equality between the races and the sexes. On another level, however, she seeks the liberation of the pure, creative, individual soul. These ideals are in conflict in *Maru:* Maru, at the highest rung in Batswana society, is ideally placed to institute reform, yet in doing so he alienates himself from the people of his society. He achieves change at the expense of leadership of his tribe. As in *Rain Clouds,* the critical flaw in the didactic purpose of *Maru* arises from Head's inability at this stage in her artistic development to unite the sphere of public life and social commitment with that of the inner life and individual fulfillment. The two dimensions of human experience are discontinuous in the novel.

To salvage something of the novel from the tensions that threaten to pull it apart, Head does some special pleading on Maru's behalf. She justifies his manipulativeness, his lying, his half-truths, and his scheming by once again pointing heavenward: Maru is in touch with the "way things are," and his actions are thereby vindicated. He is amoral, but he moves in cohesion with the inexorable pace of the universe.

A realist reading of *Maru* is unsatisfactory because the outcome of events thwarts the codes by which we judge human behavior. We are asked to judge Maru's manipulations not by human moral standards but by the transcendental principles of the universe, of destiny. A certain amount of persuasion is necessary here. Maru is not merely indulging his ego; he is obeying the "gods in his heart" (*Maru,* 8). He also deals racism a decisive blow and initiates a process of social reform that is going to be difficult to halt. We are told that he is strong enough to live with the consequences of marrying an outcast, whereas "Moleka would never have lived down the ridicule and malice and would in the end have destroyed her from embarrassment" (9).

Head is at pains to show that justice has been done. The descriptions in the opening pages are an attempt to sway the reader's judgment throughout the rest of the novel in Maru's favor by showing how exemplary and unselfish he is. He abandons all the prestige and privileges that accrue to the chieftaincy and ekes out a subsistence living in a remote, isolated rural area. Head attempts to persuade the reader to view Maru favorably because he embodies the progressive social attitudes she wishes to endorse. Racism, however, is not solved by the exemplary behavior of a single individual, however highly placed he may be. The author is forced to recognize this: "When people of Dilepe village heard about the marriage of Maru, they began to talk about him as if he had died. A Dilepe diseased prostitute explained their attitude: 'Fancy,' she said. 'He has married a Masarwa. They have no standards' " (*Maru,* 126).

For the people of Dilepe, Maru has ceased to exist. They carry out on the level of consciousness what they practice in the politics of real life: the denial of anything that threatens their racial-economic supremacy. Again, this conclusion is forced on the author. The people of Dilepe, as we saw, "knew nothing about the standards of the soul, and since Maru only lived by those standards they had never been able to make a place for him in their society" (*Maru,* 126). This is an implicit recognition of Maru's failure. Where he succeeds, however, is in his ambition to "dream the true dreams, untainted by the clamour of the world" (70). And this is the direction in which Head has been straining all along: the liberation of the individual soul and the attainment of spiritual perfection.

As the foregoing discussion has suggested, there are inherent problems in the presentation of social and political process in *Maru.* The problem of racism is perceived to lie in the hearts of the individuals who practice racism. What is required is a change of heart, and what better way to achieve this than by the example of a highly respected and highly placed individual? That this strategy does not work indicates the contradictory currents in Bessie Head's thought. Her idealism in constructing a King Cophetua–like tale is at odds with her realism in recognizing Maru's ultimate failure.[3]

This raises the question of how to interpret *Maru.* Is it to be read as realism or as allegory? On a realistic level the novel simply does not work: it is highly unlikely that two socially attractive, eligible men would compete for the affections of an outcast. And if we are to interpret the novel as conforming to the conventions of narrative realism, what are we to make of a character like Ranko, who appears and disappears like Prospero's Ariel in *The Tempest?* The novel is equally impossible as a description of the outcome of racial antagonism. The ending—the fairy-tale marriage of the prince to the misprized princess—is fanciful, to say the least.

Maru reads better as a sort of parable, a moral discourse on the evils of racial prejudice. Indeed, the power of the novel can be felt in the richly evoked social tension of the village of Dilepe, where racial prejudice is a tangible presence—perhaps an authentic reworking of the author's own experience. But the power of love, the magnetism between personalities, the communication between souls on a psychic level, the inexorable forces operating beneath the events of the workaday world, are all aspects of human experience that Head captures with vitality. And it is here that the real power of the novel lies. *Maru* succeeds as a personal, almost mystical vindication of the power of love over evil.

Head seemed to be aware of the complexities and ambiguities that the text produces and once remarked: "With all my South African experience I longed to write an enduring novel on the hideousness of racial prejudice. But I also wanted the book to be so beautiful and so magical that I, as the writer, would long to read and re-read it" (*Woman Alone,* 68). The dual intention suggested here foreshadows the duality in the novel itself: the real, historically specific problem of racism and the method of its eradication, and the fairy-tale, magical, allegorical dimension. *Maru*'s ostensible aim is to preach against racism; what it finally comes to deal with is the liberation of the individual soul.

This inconsistency reflects Head's status as an exile and as an artist in the context of the subsistence life of the Batswana peasants. As an exile she is alien; as an artist she is apart. She affirms, finally, what she knows to be an inner truth—her "otherness," her loneliness, the afflictions she shares with Margaret: "In the distance, a village proceeded with its own life but she knew not what it was. . . . She was not a part of it and belonged nowhere" (*Maru,* 93). Yet Margaret, as an artist, records village scenes, infusing her own emotions and desires into the Botswanan landscape. Like her creator she desires to belong but never expects it. All she can do is to stand outside and observe, a "true and sensitive recorder" (104).

Chapter Six
A Question of Power (1973)

A Question of Power is Bessie Head's most unusual and perplexing novel and is also widely considered to be her major work. It is a professedly autobiographical work that deals with the author's own mental break-down and subsequent recovery and renewal. Although all of Head's novels have an autobiographical dimension, *A Question of Power* is most conspicuously drawn from the life experience of the author. The central character, Elizabeth, is given a name that closely resembles the author's own, and she also shares Head's life story. She is born, we read, in a mental hospital after her mother is committed because of an affair with a black man. She is raised by a foster mother and then by a harsh mis-sionary who had "come out to save the heathen."[1] Elizabeth then joins a political party, has the misfortune to marry a womanizer, bears his child, and after the inevitable breakup of the marriage leaves for Botswana on an exit permit.

Elizabeth settles in Motabeng village, which is typically Botswanan in that it is dry and dusty and faces serious agricultural problems. It also has an international group of volunteer workers who are attempting to aid the local people in setting up agricultural projects and self-help schemes. It is in this context that Elizabeth's mental breakdown occurs. The narrative constantly switches between her tormented consciousness and the real world of the novel—the bustling village life, communal gardening, and daily activities of Elizabeth and her son, so tangibly evoked as to suggest a re-creation of the realism of *Rain Clouds*. Eliza-beth confronts in her consciousness universal powers of good and evil and struggles to attain a sense of human value amid her mental confu-sion. The novel charts the terrifying course of her breakdown, her recov-ery, and the ultimate affirmation of her belief in the importance of per-sonal humility and of the primary human values of decency, generosity, and compassion—values that provide the basis for Head's moral vision in all of her works.

According to the biographical record, then, it is clear that there is lit-tle attempt to disguise the fact that Head is telling—or more precisely, reinterpreting—her own life story in this novel. Fruitful though a biographical approach to the novel might be, this is not the approach I intend to take here. What is unusual about *A Question of Power* and what will ensure its place in future assessments of African literature, I believe, is its decisive shift of attention to what Cherry Wilhelm calls "the arena of psychic struggle" (Wilhelm, 3). It achieves this on a formal level by resolutely denying traditional narrative conventions and, accordingly, the interpretative strategies the reader traditionally employs.

Two worlds coexist on different ontological planes in the novel: there is a recognizable, social world of cooperative gardening, human interaction, and everyday events in the village; there is also an inner, psychologically constituted world, in which the logic of the nightmare, and of intuitive dream-association, predominates, and the free play of ideas is allowed to proceed. Whereas the protagonists of the earlier novels were presented with rich interior lives that they attempted to integrate with an outer social world, a different balance is struck between these two dimensions in *A Question of Power.* Elizabeth's dreams possess a certain narratological authority: they are, in fact, the very "stuff" of the text, the locus of the "real life" of the novel.

In locating the action of the novel inside the mind of a character, Head seems to be adopting a distinctively modernist strategy: the "outer" world bombards the sentient subject with a barrage of sensory impressions that must be configured by the subject's organizing intellect; the subject's ordering gaze, in other words, imposes an interpretation on a seemingly random universe.

In a radical and idiosyncratic way, however, Head interrogates the notion of a centered, ordering subject. Instead of being the organizing principle in a chaotic universe, Elizabeth's mind becomes the *site* of a monumental struggle between conflicting forces. This produces one of the central paradoxes of the novel. Head professes the novel to be autobiographical ("Elizabeth and I are one," she remarked in an interview in 1983 [*Between the Lines,* 26]), and yet, as Wilhelm has observed, "the novel is the least documentary of [her] three" (Wilhelm, 3).

Elizabeth is alienated from all of society's power structures: as a "Coloured" she is denied full selfhood in racist South Africa, as a "half-caste" she is despised in traditional African society, and as a woman she is discriminated against by the patriarchal hierarchies in both societies. In a very real sense, Elizabeth "creates" herself from the sketchy details supplied by the principal of the mission school in which she is placed as a young girl: " 'We have a full docket on you. You must be very careful. Your mother was insane. If you're not careful you'll get insane just like your mother. Your mother was a white woman. They had to lock her up, as she was having a child by the stable boy, who was a native' " (*Power,* 16).

Elizabeth has to build up any sense of unity or coherence as a person through an act of will, and bereft of the usual social support system of close friends and family and under the pressure of extreme life experiences, this fragile sense of self fragments. Elizabeth's mind is then invaded by vertiginous nightmare sequences drawn from the deepest wells of her unconscious.

The way these dreams are presented in the novel, whether one construes this as the faithful record of the author's own descent into insanity or, alternatively, as a bold experiment in narrative technique, the reader is encouraged to be a producer rather than a passive consumer of meaning. In this Head is perhaps being no more adventurous than any number of contemporary writers with postmodernist tendencies. The intriguing thing about her own attitude to the novel, however, is how explicitly she articulates the gaps and discontinuities in the text and how she actively encourages reader participation in the production of meaning. Consider what she said of the novel in an interview in 1983: "It was like a book saying now, I'll tell you as much as I can, then you sort things out. . . . [I]t's a sort of book that's written in such a way that it invites people to fill in gaps and notes where the author has left blank spaces" (*Between the Lines,* 27).

There is a palpable sense here that she is disavowing the traditional claims to authority: the author then becomes the mere conduit, so to speak, of a polyphony of discourses emanating from outside herself. The notion of "identity" that, ironically, usually provides the autobiography with a central, constitutive principle is also undermined here. Indeed, throughout the novel there is a denial of the traditional boundaries between what are conventionally conceptualized as "the real" and "the imaginary." The catalyst for this is Elizabeth's insanity, which prompts a departure from societal norms of perception. Accordingly, the transposition of her dreams into fiction produces a form of narrative that similarly abrogates the usual norms and conventions.

A key to the phantasmagoria of *A Question of Power* seems to lie in one of Elizabeth's musings shortly before she plunges into insanity: "In many ways, her slowly unfolding internal drama was far more absorbing and demanding than any drama she could encounter in Motabeng village. The insights, perceptions, fleeting images and impressions required more concentration, reflection and brooding than any other work she had ever undertaken" (*Power,* 29). This description anticipates the mental events that unfold in the novel. The drama is entirely internal, and the outside world seems to be there only to provide the images and characters that feature in Elizabeth's dreams. They impose very little of their own necessity on her: she shapes and interprets them according to her own inner necessities.

The internal drama of *A Question of Power,* in other words, has its own internal logic. It is unproductive to attempt to draw significance from the logic of cause and effect as it is taken to operate in the "normal" outside world. Events are concatenated in Elizabeth's disturbed mind by the logic of the dream, by intuitive dream association. What Head says of *Maru* applies equally well to *A Question of Power:* "My novel was built up in blinding flashes of insights into an evil that hung like the sickness of death over all black people in South Africa" (*Woman Alone,* 69). The novel does of course also testify to the inner torture of its protagonist: *A Question of Power* is as much a description of the horrors of mental breakdown as it is an exploration of the evils of racism and oppression.

What is revealing about the passage just quoted from the novel, however, is the apparent confusion between author and character. Read in one way, Head seems to be describing her own "work" in writing the novel. This establishes a pattern for the novel as a whole: Head as author repeatedly breaks through the shallow artifice of Elizabeth as character. Head is clearly expressing her own innermost, private experiences through her protagonist, and the substance of these experiences is woven into the fabric of the novel's narrative structure. This is one of the reasons that *A Question of Power* is so inaccessible to the reader. The autobiographical dimension, rendered in an often obscure personal narrative voice, makes the text intensely private.

So inaccessible is the novel that it is well-nigh impossible to construct a logical, coherent way through its lurid dream sequences. In Elizabeth's tortured mind, two men who actually live in the village of Motabeng become dream personae, Dan and Sello, who over a period of three years lead her through a series of riotous, nightmarish experiences. Sello appears in her dreams as a divine sage who sits in the corner of her room and imparts spiritual truths to her. He is a quasi-religious figure, a monk-like hallucination who first appears to be "the prophet of mankind" (*Power,* 25). In this guise he provokes Elizabeth to question her identity as an African, as a lover of humankind. Elizabeth's anxieties about her rightful place in the world, the state of her soul, her desire to ease the suffering of the oppressed peoples of Africa, and to identify with the downtrodden all surface in this period of mental breakdown in a night-marish way.

The issues that emerge clearly, and with which the dream personae Sello and Dan and other figures challenge her, are those specifically related to her experiences as an underprivileged "Coloured" growing up in South Africa. Such anxieties would have been common in the race-obsessed social system of South Africa of the 1960s and 1970s. For Eliz-abeth they cluster around her fragile sense of personal worth (a "Coloured" child was considered to be the product of an immoral alliance between black and white), her inability to identify with black consciousness and pan-Africanist groups, and her concern that she is abandoning her fellow downtrodden by elevating herself socially and materially. In Elizabeth all of these anxieties combine with the universal subconscious fear of human depravities and aberrations.

The issue that ultimately emerges from this disquiet is the question of personal power and how to use it for the betterment of humankind, hence the novel's title. Elizabeth expresses this as the underlying moti-vation for what she calls her "nightmare soul-journey": "She was talking to a monk [Sello] who had used an unnatural establishment to express a thousand and one basic principles as the ideal life because, in the heat of living, no one had come to terms with their own powers and at the same time made allowance for the powers of others" (*Power,* 35). Elizabeth considers her powers to be used positively when they are used on the basis of love for all people—"an awakening of her own powers corre-sponded to an awakening love of mankind"—and this is the affirmation that occurs again at the end of the novel: "She had fallen from the very beginning into the warm embrace of the brotherhood of man, because when a people wanted everyone to be ordinary it was just another way of saying man loved man" (*Power,* 35, 206).

The dream sequences are best elucidated by using Elizabeth's tor-tured consciousness as a starting point. The emanations of this con-sciousness are projected onto dream personae and events in a cinematic way, presenting the reader with an almost allegorical display of the evils of South African (and ultimately, human) society. Elizabeth comes to identify these evils as universal: their source is not in corrupt social sys-tems but in the inner being of each individual. The struggle between good and evil, therefore, becomes an interior, personal one, a private journey to the sources of evil.

This point is illustrated in a key passage from the novel. It identifies the issues at stake, the manner of their treatment, and the author's orientation:

> He [Sello] bent his head. There was an old man with a ring of sparse white hair. The huge bald patch shone like polished mahogany. She [Elizabeth] looked at a projection of herself. It was a minute image of a small girl with pitch-black hair. She wobbled unsteadily on her feet.
>
> "There are a set of people in my age-group and a set of people in your age-group. The first group brought about dark times. We had to dream a nobler dream, and the people of that dream belong to your age-group. Everything was wrong. Everything was evil until I broke down and cried. It is when you cry, in the blackest hour of despair, that you stumble on a source of goodness. There were a few of us who cried like that. Then we said: 'Send us perfection.' They sent you. Then we asked: 'What is perfection?' And they said: 'Love.' " (*Power,* 34)

In this extract one moves from one level of interpretation to another by the dream logic of surrealism. The author creates a character, Elizabeth, who views herself through the medium of another character, Sello, on a different ontological plane. (Elizabeth is to be taken as a "real" character. The monklike Sello is a fantasy, a projection of Elizabeth's fevered mind.) Her dream yields a context that throws her life into relief. She sees herself as a little girl. Sello then interprets the image: the first generation, of which Elizabeth's mother is a member, entrenched an iniquitous social system; Elizabeth is the progeny of that generation, who, as a symbol of race hatred and rejection, will nevertheless lead the world to recognize the power of love over evil and the moral indefensibility of racial oppression.

The real struggle in the world, according to this vision, takes place between the souls of people. All other forms of struggle are simply manifestations of inner conflict. Elizabeth muses: "People, in their souls, were forces, energies, stars, planets, universes and all kinds of swirling magic and mystery" (*Power,* 35). The souls of people are the source of both good and evil: the liberation of power that insight into self produces can lead people in either direction. Elizabeth's struggle is to use her insights and power for the cause of good: " 'Oh God,' she said, softly. 'May I never contribute to creating dead worlds, only new worlds' " (100).

Elizabeth's inner struggle is induced, like Makhaya's and Margaret's, by her dual alienation from South Africa and from the Batswana. Thus Elizabeth's affirmation of good is not made on behalf of society in general. She is unable to assert, in a partisan way, the superiority of one culture or society or political system over another and comes instead to ground her arguments on the soul of the solitary individual, the basic unit of humankind.

The monklike Sello has a "wife" whom Elizabeth describes as an "image of holiness" (*Power*, 37). Yet each projects an alter ego. From the monklike Sello steps forth a replica dressed in a brown suit. This is a shabby, spineless character who observes Elizabeth from behind his wife's alter ego, Medusa. It is the "wild-eyed Medusa" who voices Elizabeth's innermost anxieties: " 'We don't want you here. This is my land. These are my people. We keep our things to ourselves. You keep no secrets. I can do more for the poor than you could ever do' " (38).

Medusa exemplifies the narrowness, the exclusivity of African society. Elizabeth fears that she is an alien in this world. She has a European fear of "darkest Africa"—the scheming, the witchcraft, the terrors of the darkness of the African mind and continent to which she has no access. Her lodestar is her belief in the ordinary person. In advanced societies, she believes, "People had their institutions, which to a certain extent protected them from power-lusting presidents for life with the 'my people' cult. Africa had nothing, and yet, tentatively, she had been introduced to one of the most complete statements for the future a people could ever make: Be ordinary. Any assumption of greatness leads to a dog-eat-dog fight and incurs massive suffering" (*Power*, 38–39).

This is, to a certain extent, a Eurocentric fear of the lack of institutional controls in African societies. Yet in Elizabeth's vision of a new Africa, the ordinary people can be this control, "because when a people wanted everyone to be ordinary it was just another way of saying man loved man" (*Power*, 206). In her nightmares, Elizabeth explores the alternatives available to Africa. Since she has been a victim of both white and black oppression, her experience is her guide to an unprejudiced social system. She therefore works insistently from her own personal experiences, fears, and intuitions toward a broader conception of a better society. In the microcosm of her consciousness is contained the macrocosm in which the broad social struggles and universal issues are played out.

Sello the monk is dominated by Medusa and later by the supreme male ego, Dan: "It was the quality of his [Sello's] soul-power which placed him at a disadvantage in these circumstances. She [Elizabeth] knew it because basically she was composed of the same material. It was, in its final state, passive, inactive, impersonal. It was linked in some way to the creative function, the dreamer of new dreams; and the essential ingredient in creativity is to create and let the dream fly away with a soft hand and heart" (*Power,* 42).

A number of strands in Head's thought are drawn together here. The antithesis she outlines—the creative, passive dreamer and the aggressive, power-hungry self-seeker—also underlies the characterization in her earlier novels. Makhaya is opposed by Matenge and Joas Tsepe. Maru and Margaret are opposed by the people of Dilepe and, in a different way, by Moleka. Elizabeth's description of Sello (and of herself) easily could have been one of Maru and, to a lesser extent, of Makhaya and Margaret. This suggests a continuity in Head's thoughts and concerns. She consistently creates protagonists who live creatively and seek creative political alternatives. This, of course, is largely a function of her own context: she is a person whose work, in her own words, "created new worlds out of nothing" (*Woman Alone,* 28).

She does this on two (related) levels: as a writer she constantly looks forward by viewing the "viciousnesses of South Africa's political kingdom" in "meaningful relation to South Africa's future" (Ravenscroft, 174); as a vegetable gardener she attempts to grow food for survival in barren, hostile soil. She conceptualizes the politically progressive person as a passive dreamer, a prophet who points the way and then retires from public view. Because of the passivity of such figures, they are easily crushed. Makhaya comes within a hair's breadth of being crushed by the system—in both South Africa and Botswana. Margaret has no active response to her victimization (other than to record it privately in her art) and is rescued only by the intervention of her foster mother and later by Maru. Maru is best equipped to counter his opponents and is therefore possibly Head's answer to the vulnerability of the prophet figure. And yet he does this by manipulation, by prescience, rather than by brute force of will.

What is common to Head's novels is a belief in the ability of individual people to initiate broad social change. If progress is to come at all it will be put into motion by a strong-willed, intelligent, near-divine leader. The common people will gape in a mystified fashion at the direction suggested, resist at first, and then slowly move forward. This conceptualization of the nature of change suggests an inconsistency in Head's thought: she claims to put her faith in the common man and yet at the same time denies him the capacity to break out of his traditional ways. (This point will be discussed in more detail later.)

Head projects her idea of an African future through the character Sello, who says: " 'I hear the beginnings of a great symphony, a complete statement for the future about the dignity of man, where none is

high and none is low but all are equal' " (*Power,* 63). All the thoughts
that are expressed in the dream passages emanate from Elizabeth's consciousness. The inconsistency in Sello (now good, now evil) and the conflict between him and Medusa and Dan, as well as with Elizabeth, are
actually conflicts within the troubled consciousness of the protagonist—
and before her, the author.

Indeed, it is interesting to observe that a significant number of the
characters who feature in Head's novels have schizophrenic tendencies.
In *The Cardinals,* Johnny is both solicitous toward Mouse and violently
abusive of her. Makhaya in *When Rain Clouds Gather* is projected alter-
nately as a pacifist and as a man with an uncontrollable temper. In
Maru, Maru and Moleka both veer between tranquillity and murderous
rage, and their partners, we are told, "alternated happiness with misery,"
finding themselves "tossed about this way and that on permanently
restless seas" (*Maru,* 115). And in an early story entitled "Tao"[2]—which,
incidentally, reads like a dry run for both *Rain Clouds* and *Maru*—the
titular character is both a sensitive and immensely attractive man and
also a manipulative demagogue and opportunistic political animal.
Intriguingly, the vantage point of these contradictory observations is
that of a young woman teacher, new to the area and naive and impressionable. Consider also the character described in an early piece entitled
"The Green Tree." The last paragraph of the piece is worth quoting to
demonstrate the tremendous struggle he wages against his own uncontrollable emotions:

> Everything I have wanted I have had through force, cunning or calcula-
> tion. Now, I lie awake at night, craving something I fear to possess. Just
> as our cattle would go insane at the unaccustomed sight of a hill covered
> with greenery; so do I live in fear of the body of a woman that has been
> transplanted by upheaval and uncertain conditions into harsh and barren
> soil. Sometimes I feel it beneath me; cool, like the depths of the night
> when the moon brings the pale light of heaven to earth and makes the
> dust shimmer like gold. Then my hands reach out to crush the life out of
> the thing that torments me.[3]

It is hard to resist reading strong autobiographical messages into passages like this, saturated as they are with the contradictory impulses of
their author and tinged with elements of wish fulfillment. Indeed, this is
a feature of much of Head's early writing—a compulsion to work
through sublimated emotions that fight their way to the surface of her
consciousness.

A Question of Power abounds in passages that signal a projection through Elizabeth of the author's own fears and prejudices. Elizabeth displays a strong Afrophobic element in her character. Sello, the dream projection of her obsessive imagination, expresses her own anxieties: " 'The surface of life here is narrow, stifling and full of petty prejudice. It is a world with the power to turn in on itself and keep its own secrets' " (*Power,* 63). The position of the leader in this kind of society is fragile and tenuous. Sello remarks: " 'They don't give a damn for my status as spiritual superman. There's no such thing as the superman here, that is, if I'm living as a man I'm human and fallible like everyone else. People who have been despised for so long know evil at its roots' " (63).

The twists and turns, reverses in logic, and inconsistency in thought that this passage demonstrates is typical of the dream passages throughout the novel. Authorial control of characterization, perspective, and even tense is abandoned as the debate goes back and forth in Elizabeth's fevered mind. (What is the role of the leader? Will he have the power to lead the people out of their narrow, stifling traditions? Should there be a leader at all?) What emerges is a sense of tension between Head's notion of the superleader, the prophet of change, and her belief in the common people. Is the leader going to act on the consensus of the people, or does he or she lead them blindfolded?

Elizabeth also ponders the problem of the black nationalist power seeker: "When someone says 'my people' with a specific stress on the blackness of those people, they are after kingdoms and permanently child-like slaves. 'The people' are never going to rise above the status of 'the people.' They are going to be told what is good for them by the 'mother' and the 'father' " (*Power,* 63). Head clearly finds degrading the paternalism of the traditional tribal chief. It would thwart the aspirations of the people and keep them in a permanently childlike state. This antitribal theme is given strong expression in her two earlier Botswana novels and is carried over into *A Question of Power* on a more abstract plane.

Religion comes under equally vehement attack. God and religion are seen as further distractions from the real issues. Buddhism, for example, was too distant from the immediate, practical needs of the people: "The meditations under the Bodhi tree were as precarious and uncertain as any venture in life. God was no security for the soul" (*Power,* 65). Elizabeth turns away from the lacunae produced by religious mysticism and moves toward a form of African realism: "The real battlefront was living people, their personalities, their treatment of each other. A real, living battle of jealousy, hate and greed was more easily understood and resolved under pressure than soaring, mystical flights of the soul" (66).

This in some ways anticipates the more socially oriented work that Head produced after *A Question of Power.* Yet the notion of everything finally being reduced to basic human nature, to the exigencies of day-to-day life, is expressed in *Rain Clouds* as well: "It seemed to Makhaya far preferable for Africa if it did without Christianity and Christian double-talk, fat priests, golden images, and looked around at all the thin naked old men who sat under trees weaving baskets with shaking hands. People could do without religions and Gods who died for the sins of the world and thereby left men without any feeling of self-responsibility for the crimes they committed" (*Rain Clouds,* 134). Here, however, religion is given a specific historical context. Head is rejecting a particular form of Christianity—the fraudulent form it took under the missionaries who were the vanguard of the colonizers. In *A Question of Power* her thought moves in a more general way away from the supernatural—in which man could divest himself of human responsibility—and toward a more people-centered moral order.

The "real world" of the novel centers on Elizabeth's involvement in communal gardening. Gardening is the physical counterpart to her mental struggle to adapt to her environment. It symbolizes her struggle to overcome alienation. Food production on a cooperative basis incorporates her aspirations of sharing with the community and coming to terms with the harsh environment. In it there is also a sense of the integration of the natural and the social worlds. Walking down "the rough, shady road" to the vegetable gardens, Elizabeth ponders the deeper significance of this activity: "It is impossible to become a vegetable gardener without at the same time coming into contact with the wonderful strangeness of human nature. Every man and woman is, in some way, an amateur gardener at heart and vegetables are really the central part of the daily diet" (*Power,* 72).

In the phrase "Cape Gooseberry" (Elizabeth and her fellow gardener Kenosi introduce the Cape Gooseberry to the village) all of these aspects are brought into a symbolic focus: "The work had a melody like that—a complete stranger like the Cape Gooseberry settled down and became a part of the village life of Motabeng. It loved the hot, dry Botswana summers as they were a replica of the Mediterranean summers of its home in the Cape" (*Power,* 153).

The "Cape Gooseberry" (which becomes Elizabeth's nickname) is of course a symbol of Head's own exile and resettlement. It also symbolizes the progressiveness of the multinational Motabeng community and the Batswana themselves—their willingness to try something new to break the stranglehold the semidesert conditions have on rural Botswana. In all of this there is a resilience and a sense of commitment, a determination to take root and to allow the "shattered little bits" to come together again (*Woman Alone,* 30).

On an economic level, cooperative gardening is a possible way out of the stagnant subsistence economy of the Batswana. Elizabeth is aware of how tentative and fragile the whole project is, however. Not so Camilla, the Danish woman who supervises work in the cooperative garden: "She could not even begin to see the extreme delicacy and precariousness of the experiment, that they were young men who had had no future and were suddenly being given one, and that they took Eugene's offer very seriously" (*Power,* 76).

The novel deals with the Danish community and their relations with the local Batswana at some length. Camilla represents the insensitive arrogance of the majority of these people. She reduces the gardeners to "humiliated little boys" (*Power,* 76). She never looks beyond their black skins to see "the shades and shadows of life on black people's faces" but treats them instead as "objects of permanent idiocy" (82, 76). Elizabeth she treats in a patronizing way, arrogantly asserting her superiority, culturally and intellectually. For Elizabeth she epitomizes the mindless prattler who never stops to consider the feelings of others: "All life had to stop and turn towards her" (75). She has only the doubtful authority of a member of the white, educated elite in Africa and not the smallest understanding of broader issues: "Her voice had an insistent command to it, yet it was no command of life. It was a scatter-brained assertion of self-importance" (75).

Camilla takes for granted the idiocy of everyone around her, and Elizabeth is not exempt from this treatment. As the author wryly notes, "Elizabeth was naturally an imbecile about the wonders of nature, and this Camilla had to make amends for on the mile-long journey to her home" (*Power,* 76). This is an example of what Elizabeth understands as her lack of "command of life" (75). Like the white people of South Africa, she seems to want to deny the access of the black person to things of beauty. Head commented acerbically on this aspect of black oppression: "In South Africa the white man took even the air away from us—it was his air and his birds and his land. In Botswana, I have a little bird outside my window every day. No one laid any particular claim to him, so I am able to confide, to the whole world, that he sings like this, and he sings like that, without some white man or woman snickering behind my ear: 'Why, you people don't appreciate things like *that*!' " (*Woman Alone,* 27–28).

Head's criticism of the Danish volunteer community rests on the observation that they view Botswana through the eyes of the culture in which they have been brought up. A black student's hesitation to embrace wholeheartedly a field of new ideas is interpreted as stupidity or laziness. Elizabeth sees the heart of the Batswana: "There's a dismal life behind them of starvation and years and years of drought when there was no food, no hope, no anything. There's a magical world ahead of them with the despair and drudgery of semi-desert agriculture alleviated by knowledge. When people stumble upon magic they study it very closely, because all living people are, at heart, amateur scientists and inventors. Why must racialists make an exception of the black man?" (*Power,* 82–83).

In his study of French peasant life, *Pig Earth,* John Berger makes a similar observation: "When a peasant resists the introduction of a new technique or method of working, it is not because he cannot see its possible advantages—his conservatism is neither blind nor lazy—but because he believes that these advantages cannot, by the nature of things, be guaranteed, and that, should they fail, he will then be cut off alone and isolated from the routine of survival."[4] What Berger points to is the essentially contrary views of time, of continuity, that the urban and the rural peasant communities hold. Berger identifies the peasant view of time as cyclical: "Inexhaustibly committed to wresting a life from the earth, bound to the present of endless work, the peasant nevertheless sees life as an interlude. This is confirmed by his daily familiarity with the cycle of birth, life and death" (Berger, 200). A peasant culture is therefore, in Berger's terms, a "culture of survival" as opposed to an urban "culture of progress" (204).

The Danish community at Motabeng are exponents of the latter culture: they have a linear sense of time and a belief in progress. The future lies open to progress through the application of technology and knowledge; humankind is moving in a linear fashion from a position of ignorance and poverty toward a point where its prosperity will be assured. For the Batswana peasant this view is totally alien, and Head, through Elizabeth, expresses her understanding of, and solidarity with, the ordinary Batswana man or woman by holding up to critical scrutiny the arrogance of European interlopers like Camilla.

Part 2 of the novel centers on the dream figure Dan. Dan is presented in Elizabeth's consciousness as a symbol of black male virility. He challenges her sexuality as well as her racial designation as "Coloured." The kind of power being explored through Dan is a personal power, power as a sexual being, power as a member of a race group. What seems to both fascinate and repel Elizabeth is the relentlessly acquisitive, aggressive, manipulative male ego. All Dan does is motivated by entirely selfish desires: he is self-centered, callous, and arrogant and has an array of mistresses whom he gloatingly parades before Elizabeth.

In the figure Dan, then, appears to be concentrated all of Elizabeth's anxieties about her own sexual inadequacies as well as her fear of unbridled sexual desire and perversion. Dan repeatedly taunts her with such statements as "You are supposed to feel jealous. You are inferior as a Coloured. You haven't got what that girl has got" (*Power,* 127). As part 2 of the novel unfolds, Dan floods her consciousness with lurid scenes of sexual activity, and these ultimately cause her to lose her grip on reality and succumb to a complete nervous collapse.

The significance of Elizabeth's nightmares is that in them she is forced to plumb the depths of humanity's depravity, its lust for power, its arrogance, its sexual craving. In her nightmares the figures Medusa and Dan personify all of the negative dimensions of human nature. Throughout, Sello is her guide, her inner intuitive sense of good, of humanity and justice, that guides her through the horror toward an ultimate affirmation of what she calls "the brotherhood of man" (*Power,* 206).

The psychologically exhausting process of Elizabeth's inner struggle threatens to engulf her entirely. More than once she contemplates suicide. In each case the outside world intervenes and restores some of the balance. What really sustains her, however, is her inner sense of good: "It wasn't any kind of physical stamina that kept her going, but a vague, instinctive pattern of normal human decencies combined with the work she did, the people she met each day and the unfolding of a project with exciting inventive possibilities. But a person eventually becomes a replica of the inner demons he battles with" (149–50).

What is interesting is Elizabeth's claim that the "inner demons" are an external force, not simply the product of a fevered mind. At the height of her mental illness her inner torment causes her to take action in the real world. She pins a signed note to the wall of the Motabeng post office stating, "SELLO IS A FILTHY PERVERT WHO SLEEPS WITH HIS DAUGHTER" (*Power,* 175). At this point Elizabeth has completely lost her sense of real and unreal. Her inner nightmares have become so compelling that she can no longer separate them from events in the outside world. Evil is presented here as an external force, independent of one's mind and acting on one in a destructive way.

This understanding of evil introduces perplexing details into the text. The monklike Sello, who sits in the corner of Elizabeth's room, "sounds off" a loud "ting" whenever either Elizabeth or whoever is visiting her makes a good point. This occurs when the American volunteer worker Tom is visiting her, and he actually looks around the room in a startled way (*Power*, 24). Here the "unreal" interpenetrates the "real." Another example of this is when Elizabeth has a nightmare during which Sello disposes of the Medusa figure. The next morning Elizabeth's son finds footprints and a heap of charcoal dust in the center of the room.

These events illustrate Elizabeth's claim that she is being assaulted by "a powerful invasion force from outside" (*Power*, 145). But how is the reader to interpret them? They reveal, I believe, a marked indeterminacy in the ontological footing of the novel. This indeterminacy stems directly from Head's authorial confusion as to *what* happened during her own mental breakdown and *how* to render it within the pages of a novel. Interviews with Head suggest that the author was never able to achieve clarity about what happened to her during her mental breakdown. In 1983 she made the following cryptic comment: "But sometimes you wonder how people distanced from you, who haven't experienced it, would interpret such a situation. Would they say that the writer of *A Question of Power* was outright insane, or would they say that her torturers were up to something, that there was something that they were after?" (*Between the Lines*, 25).

Toward the end of her life, then, she still appeared to be confused about what took place in her tortured consciousness (and was therefore imaginary) and what, on the other hand, took place in the world around her (independently observable reality). Consider the confusion of the following response to a question about the background to *A Question of Power:* "I say it is probable—since I believe in reincarnation—I was under the assumption that I was reliving some of my past lives. The men Sello and Dan were not totally unknown to me in the sense that it was possible that they were some part of my past life. But I'm as doubtful as everybody else, because the book's continually written with gaps and blanks" (*Between the Lines*, 26).

It is true that some of these imponderables were present in *Maru*. Indeed, the narrative style of *Maru* in some ways anticipates the later novel, especially where the author deals with the "realm of the soul" in which the spiritual struggle between Maru, Margaret, and Moleka takes place. In *Maru,* however, the author does finally attempt (unsatisfactorily, I have argued) to knit the "real world" and the "realm of the soul" together into a cohesive whole. In *A Question of Power* there is no such attempt at unity: what Head attempts through her protagonist Elizabeth is an exploration of the experiences of her life and an investigation into what they signify in the greater context of an Africa in transition. The novel calls on the reader to abandon conventional expectations to strike directly toward its heart. The invitation, in other words, is to plunge into the nightmare reality of Elizabeth's consciousness, to experience at a narrative level the real struggle of the protagonist, and to emerge finally, with her, exhausted but spiritually renewed.

In *Rain Clouds,* Makhaya's struggle is to reconcile his material existence with his inner life. His life is conceived to be channeled by his experience in these two dimensions. He acts in the real world, and the world in turn provokes an inner reaction. The two realms are finally brought into accord. With *Maru,* the stress is more on the inner self. Yet Maru succeeds in his ideals only when he has brought the outside world into harmony with his inward desires. In *A Question of Power* the relationship between inner and outer is at its most tenuous. There is virtually no causal connection between reality and Elizabeth's nightmares. At one point she questions this disjunction: "How did it all happen here, in so unsuspecting a climate, these silent, tortured, universal questions of power and love; of loss and sacrifice?" (*Power,* 97–98).

Elizabeth's struggle is entirely internal: she undergoes an experience of evil at its roots and emerges with an affirmation of "good." At the end of the novel, Elizabeth describes her "journey into hell": "Maybe, the work she and Sello had done together had introduced a softness and tenderness into mankind's history. . . . They had perfected together the ideal of sharing everything and then perfectly shared everything with all mankind" (*Power,* 202).

In broad terms this is a kind of affirmation similar to those made in the earlier novels. The "ideal of sharing everything" is at the basis of Head's moral perspective. And she sees this principle as applying to every aspect of human life: thus, in the economic sphere, for example, cooperatives are the expression of this communal spirit. Her mental breakdown occurs in the process of testing these ideals. But she has withstood the assaults on her sense of human value and has emerged revitalized: "[F]rom the degradation and destruction of her life had arisen a still, lofty serenity of soul nothing could shake" (*Power,* 202).

Chapter Seven
Putting Down Roots

Although Head's commitment to her adopted country was formally recip-
rocated only with the granting of Botswanan citizenship to her in February 1979, the period of the early and middle seventies saw Head
engaging more constructively with the rich social life of the country
and, in particular, of Serowe. Prompted by a request from Ken MacKenzie, whom Head had known as the Cape Town editor of *Drum,* to do
some research on his great-grandfather the missionary John MacKenzie,
she started sifting through the colonial history of Botswana and immediately came upon the legendary Khama III (more commonly called
Khama the Great). At about the same time that she was immersing herself in Botswanan history, Giles Gordon, her literary agent, came up
with the idea that she write a book along the lines of Jan Myrdal's *Report
from a Chinese Village* (1963) and Ronald Blythe's *Akenfield: Portrait of an
English Village* (1969), both published by Penguin.

Head's research into the local history of Serowe uncovered three out-
standing figures: Khama the Great, Tshekedi Khama, and Patrick van
Rensburg. These figures had all demonstrated the vision and stature to
rally societies around them and hence to shape history, and she decided
to structure what she had begun to call her "Serowe book" around them.
A significant part of her research consisted of interviews with local people, and here she was to rely on the invaluable help of her gardening
friend Bosele Sianana, who had acquired a working knowledge of English. The two of them sought out especially the older members of the
community, who could remember (or thought they could remember)
the old days when customs were not as adulterated by modern innovations as they were by the 1970s.

The material that emerged from this research issued in two principal
forms: the documentary, social-history format of what eventually
appeared as *Serowe: Village of the Rain Wind* (1981) and the fictional tales
contained in *The Collector of Treasures and Other Botswana Village Tales*
(1977). As the discrepancy in the publication dates of these two texts
suggests, Head had trouble getting *Serowe* into print. After protracted
wrangles with various publishers in South Africa, England, and Amer-

ica, she abruptly terminated her relationship with Giles Gordon, Patrick Cullinan, (whose Bateleur Press had made an offer to publish *Serowe* and the collection of stories locally) and ultimately, Reg Davis-Poynter, who had published *A Question of Power* and had contracted to publish *Serowe*. Gillian Eilersen describes Head's wrong-footed and ruinous behavior very succinctly: "Relentlessly, brick by brick, Bessie had been pulling down the framework for all her creative expression. Now the whole structure was crashing round her ears. Though she did not see it like that, there was no one to blame but herself" (Eilersen, 181). As it happened, *The Collector of Treasures* was to find publishers fairly readily (Heinemann in London and David Philip in Cape Town), while *Serowe* was destined for years to be sent from publisher to publisher, eliciting usually guarded praise but not for some time a firm offer of publication.

In the meantime, Head's renown as a writer was beginning to yield other, unexpected results. In April 1976 the University of Botswana hosted its first Writers' Workshop and she was invited to speak. Among the other writers invited were the academic and writer Stephen Gray, the emerging poet Sipho Sepamla, and the short-story writer Mbulelo Mzamane. Head was also sought out at this time by Mary Benson, who was spending some months in Botswana and wanted to establish contact with her. The attention Head received from these writers and the generous response to the paper she nervously presented at the conference ("Some Notes on Novel Writing," reprinted in *A Woman Alone*) must have given her a welcome fresh perspective on the private obsessions and troubles that had taken on such crushing proportions in her isolation in Serowe.

An event of great consequence to her development as a thinker and writer was her introduction to the pioneer black South African writer Sol T. Plaatje. Stephen Gray offered at the conference to send her a copy of his novel *Mhudi* (1930), and on receiving the book she responded rapturously to Plaatje's broad, humane vision. As we shall see in chapter 10, there can be little doubt that Plaatje's epic historical sweep and concern with providing a corrective view on African history had a material influence on the shaping of Head's own work.

That the world was opening up to her was signaled in a quite dramatic way by the offer in July 1977 of a scholarship to attend the International Writing Program at the University of Iowa. This would be her first experience of air travel and her first encounter with other international writers. There were several hurdles to overcome, chief among which was that, as a stateless person, she had no travel documents. The

American Embassy issued her with temporary documents, however, and she left for New York via Lusaka and London.

One of the most important aspects of this unexpected trip to America was the well-stocked libraries she was able to use for her research into southern African history. That she had been awarded a generous grant also allowed her for the first time in her life to live and work quietly and steadily without the constant anxiety of having to find money to provide for her and Howard. A sketch she later wrote about this period, "Some Happy Memories of Iowa" (1987), as its title suggests, reflects the tranquillity she experienced during her visit. She built a routine that was "quiet" and "predictable" and that was only momentarily shaken when she had to navigate her way around the vast university library:

> I was researching a historical novel and had partly done some of the work at home. My next chore was to visit the university library. The first time I did so I was thrown off balance. A young man stood behind a counter writing on a card. He looked up briefly. "Can I help you?" he asked.
> My story was a long one. I began: "I am doing research for a historical novel on Southern Africa . . ."
> "Africa," he said. "Fifth floor." And he went back to writing on the card again. I stood there shaking with fright. I am used to libraries where the librarian holds your hand and finds books for you. The young man was completely uninterested in my existence. I took my courage in both hands and took the lift to the fifth floor. Never had I seen such a desolation of solitude, silence, and books. . . . In the words of Jorge Luis Borges: "Paradise is a library." The fifth floor became that paradise to me. (*Woman Alone*, 92–93)

America opened up other opportunities for her. Several North American–based academics and writers contacted her, among them the South African Cecil Abrahams, relative of the novelist Peter Abrahams, and the writer Margaret Walker. Walker had read Head's novels and invited her to give a guest lecture at Jackson State University, where Walker was head of the Department of Black Studies. Head took up this offer and also appeared on television and attended other engagements.

Ironically, at this time of almost unprecedented success she received an official letter from the Botswanan Department of Home Affairs notifying her that her application for Botswanan citizenship had been turned down. Head took this news badly: at a time when she was abroad representing her adopted country, the country had rejected her. This bad news was balanced, however, by the appearance in print of *The*

Collector of Treasures, published simultaneously in London and Cape Town. Almost uniformly well received, the collection must have allowed her to put still further distance between her and *A Question of Power,* the appearance of which was clouded in controversy and dispute. On her way back to Botswana she spent a day in London, where more disputes about publishing awaited her. Rex Collings was interested in publishing *Serowe: Village of the Rain Wind* in a substantially altered form, an arrangement in which Head was not interested.

Returning to Botswana was something of an anticlimax. From the great distance of the United States, researching southern African history for much of the four-month scholarship in a well-stocked university library, Head must have felt an affinity with Africa and in particular with Botswana. The refusal of citizenship, however, and the anticlimax that inevitably accompanied her return home after such a momentous trip made her feel unsettled and unhappy once more. Eilersen describes her situation very aptly: "In America she had perforce represented the country, not only on a formal level because it was the country of her residence, but also on a cultural level. She had explained her views of village life, the cooperative movement and most of all the country's historical background. In return she had been told that she was of no use to Botswana. She was a refugee, without any political rights, and she would remain one. She made the firm decision never to apply for citizenship again" (Eilersen, 217).

What followed just over a year later came as a complete surprise to her. Out of the blue, without having reapplied, she was suddenly granted Botswanan citizenship. This settled for her the ongoing issue of repatriation. Although she would for the rest of her life feel the tug of contrary emotions about being a resident of a remote village in Africa, the urgency of her desire to relocate died away. Her adopted country now became her adoptive country, and she would henceforth unambiguously be Botswana's foremost literary representative.

Shortly before this she had received another piece of welcome and unexpected news: Heinemann had accepted *Serowe: Village of the Rain Wind* for publication. These two unexpected events, barely a month apart, meant that she had at last turned the corner. For *Serowe* was for her more than just another published work; it was her act of recompense to a community that had provided her with a home when there was nowhere else to turn. To be sure, the process of mutual acceptance had been a fraught and protracted one, but as she herself was to remark a few years later, "I need a quiet backwater and a sense of living as though I am barely alive on the earth, treading a small, careful pathway through life," and Botswana provided just such a milieu (*Woman Alone,* 77).

The same year, 1979, saw her on the move again. A German cultural group contacted her and asked to participate in what became the Berlin Festival of World Cultures. Armed with her new Botswanan passport, which made travel not only logistically but also psychologically easier, she left in June for Berlin, where she presented a paper entitled "Social and Political Pressures That Shape Literature in Southern Africa." Despite the emotional agitation that had immediately preceded the granting of citizenship earlier in the year, the paper is a balanced and coherent overview of southern African history and of the place of her work in this broader framework. In it she articulates very precisely the reasons for her inability to write in South Africa: "I was born in South Africa and that is synonymous with saying that one is born into a very brutal world—if one is black. . . . A sense of history was totally absent in me and it was as if, far back in history, thieves had stolen the land and were so anxious to cover up all traces of the theft that correspondingly, all traces of the true history have been obliterated" (*Woman Alone,* 66). Adding that as the "main function of a writer is to make life magical and to communicate a sense of wonder," she "found the South African situation so evil that it was impossible . . . to deal with, in creative terms" (67). In Botswana, by contrast, the "people of the land were never exposed to or broken by the sheer stark horror of white domination. They kept on dreaming as from ancient times and they kept alive the portrait of ancient Africa. It was this peaceful world of black people simply dreaming in their own skins that I began to slowly absorb into my own life" (72).

Eilersen notes that despite "small successes" Head did not fit in very well in Berlin: "The discovery of an element of ruralism in Iowa had made her visit to America enjoyable for her. Nowhere could anything similar be found in Berlin. The extreme materialism of Europe horrified her" (Eilersen, 229). There were other undercurrents causing unease for Head at the conference. Although she met up again with Dennis Brutus, her old friend from Cape Town and Port Elizabeth, their meeting did not rekindle mutual affection and interests; they had grown apart. There was also discord among the organizers of the conference, and one was fired before the conference ended.

Upon returning to Serowe, she once again took up her work on the neglected "Khama novel." With the assistance of a British Council grant, she was able to stay almost a year in Gaborone, much of which

she spent at the University of Botswana library. She was again interrupted in her research by an invitation to attend an international conference, this time in Denmark. She and the Kenyan writer Ngugi wa
Thiong'o were among the 200 delegates who attended the Danish
Library Association conference marking the association's 75th anniver-
sary. After delivering a short address to the conference in Copenhagen,
she was able to spend some time elsewhere in the country, giving lec-
tures to students at various tertiary institutions and being interviewed
on television.

Eilersen notes that one of the key issues to emerge during this trip
was feminism, which had become a powerful social and intellectual
movement in Denmark: "The women's group she was asked to address
was more feminist in tone than any other she had encountered and she
was constantly being called upon to express her own views on that subject. Her refusal to take a radical stand made some of her listeners
annoyed, especially as many saw her as one of the foremost African fem-
inists" (Eilersen, 237). Some years later she was to state her position on
the issue. Echoing such illustrious South African forebears as Olive
Schreiner and Nadine Gordimer, she insisted that writers are androgy-
nous beings: "Writing is not a male/female occupation. My femaleness
was never a problem to me, not now, not in our age. More than a century ago, a few pioneer women writers, writing fearfully under male
pseudonyms, established that women writers were brilliant thinkers too,
on a par with men. I do not have to be a feminist. The world of the
intellect is impersonal, sexless" (*Woman Alone,* 95).

Bessie Head was entering the final phase of her life. Although she
would still experience some of the turbulence in her relationships with
others that had plagued her life and almost blighted her career as a
writer, she had found a new equilibrium. When *Serowe: Village of the Rain
Wind* finally appeared in June 1981, she was granted her wish to receive
and distribute to her collaborators free copies of the book. The book was
quietly received, although it did gain some respectful attention in
Britain, where it was reviewed in the *Listener* and in *New Society.* In
Serowe, however, its appearance was more deeply registered. Head
made good on her promise to issue a free copy to each of her inter-
viewees, and several of them recorded their appreciation in comments
and letters that she later received.

She continued to receive invitations to speak at various events
abroad. In this way she traveled to Holland, Nigeria, and neighboring
Zimbabwe, where she encountered some hostility to her work: "A lec-

turer in Nigeria said he found a coolness and detachment in my writing that was un-African. . . . A Zimbabwe student said to me: 'We read Ngugi, Achebe, Ayi Kwei Armah, and we find things there that we can identify with. But with you we are disorientated and thrown into Western literature' " (*Between the Lines,* 12). Her response to these criticisms paralleled the earlier one in relation to her questionable allegiance to feminism: "Before one is necessarily black, one is first a storyteller— mankind's storyteller," she observed (12).

Early in 1983 Head received a letter from Michael Chapman, then consulting editor for the Johannesburg-based publisher Ad. Donker, asking if she was working on anything that would fit into a new series on women's writing that the firm was planning. Head immediately saw the opportunity to get her languishing Khama novel completed and into print and responded positively. She was given the deadline of the end of the year, and it appeared that at last she had the incentive she needed to complete the book she had been working on for nearly a decade.

Before *A Bewitched Crossroad* finally appeared in October 1984, Head made one more trip abroad, this time to Australia. Her increasing stature in the literary world was reflected in the fact that she now appeared alongside major literary figures from regions other than Africa, Angela Carter, Salman Rushdie, and Bruce Chatwin among them. And although she was little known on her arrival, she was to record with great satisfaction how the copies of her texts available at the event were quickly snapped up. Eilersen quotes her as observing later that the audience "quietly fell in love" with her and that it was "the most tender and beautiful thing" that had ever happened to her (Eilersen, 271).

Having at last put her Khama novel to rest, Head was in a position to begin something new. In May 1984 her agent contacted her with the news that Heinemann was interested in commissioning her to write her autobiography. Head responded promptly, asking her agent to set up a contract. She also immediately started planning the work, toying with the title "Living on an Horizon" and proposing various ideas. An area she was anxious about from the outset, however, was the South African part of her life. Eilersen notes that she made the following remark to her agent: "Other countries honour their citizens and help them find their relatives but not white South Africa. I am as anxious to avoid any knowledge of my mother's white relatives as they were anxious to destroy my mother and disown me. . . . Can the early beginnings remain as spare as that?" (Eilersen, 278).

Clearly, the wounds from her childhood had not healed. It is worth recalling the words of one of her white relatives, her uncle Kenneth Birch, on the matter: "I do not think my niece was incapable of finding the Birch family. . . . She knew her eldest uncle, Walter (Ben), the then main family representative, was highly unsympathetic, with the implication therefore that the rest of the family were not interested" (Birch, 16). It may have been trepidation about revisiting a painful past that caused the autobiography to falter. In any event, a proposed date of completion, September 1986, was set with Heinemann, and Head received an advance. Eilersen records that Head did write to the welfare society in Pietermaritzburg, asking for detailed information about her background, but received no reply.

At around this time she was becoming more and more quiet and withdrawn. Major events like her divorce, which finally occurred when Harold visited Gaborone, came and went with little comment. When I visited her in January 1985 she was restrained and polite but refused an interview, and I left with the impression that she was confused and unwell. At about this time she began to drink heavily. She had always had a capacity to drink vast amounts of beer, but now beer was replaced by brandy and gin, and according to Eilersen, by March 1986 she was consuming about a bottle a day. Her skin began taking on a yellowish hue and the doctor diagnosed hepatitis. Head refused to take his advice that she be hospitalized immediately and instead returned home. A friend arrived to see how she was on the afternoon of 16 April and found her weak and helpless. An ambulance was called and Head was taken to the hospital, where she later slipped into a coma. By late afternoon on 17 April her breathing gradually faded away, and she died.

The event she had been anticipating soon after her arrival in Botswana some 20 years earlier had finally come to pass. With what might have been extraordinary prescience she had said some years earlier: "I am trying to gather several threads together to create a feeling of continuity in my work . . . to finally record some of the kind of welding I felt on coming to a country like Botswana. It was like finding roots and these roots really go back, for me, to the old tribal way of life and its slow courtesies. . . . So this final work I am on will have the effect of rounding off my southern African experience. I think I will then let it fall asleep in my mind."[1]

Chapter Eight
The Collector of Treasures (1977)

The stories of *The Collector of Treasures* deal with the issues that emerge in Botswanan village life: tribal history, the missionaries, religious conflict, witchcraft, rising illegitimacy, and throughout, problems that women encounter in society. Each of these issues is central to a particular story. Yet each story is also deftly allusive and evokes vividly and richly the sense of a real, living, bustling village struggling to cope with the intrusion of new forces into the traditional social fabric.

The stories are arranged in a careful sequence: they reenact, as it were, the historical process from ancient, mythical times, through the subsequent arrival of a new culture and the conflict with tradition, and on to contemporary times, in which the breakdown of the family and all the other problems experienced by a society in upheaval are dealt with. Head draws a complete portrait of the village, each story being a part of the composite whole and giving the impression of overlapping with others around it. Her storytelling encompasses the minute, the particular, the details of an event in a person's life as well as an awareness of the greater social context.

Another important dimension to the stories of *The Collector of Treasures*—signaled by the collection's subtitle, *and Other Botswana Village Tales*—is their engagement with the oral culture of the traditional African village of Serowe. This tradition takes both ancient and modern forms: Serowe possesses venerable old "tribal historians," but it is also characterized by a contemporary ethos of village gossip and storytelling. The historical range of Head's stories takes in this multifaceted nature of Serowan oral culture.

"The Deep River: A Story of Ancient Tribal Migration"

As its title suggests, the first story in the collection deals with an important aspect of oral culture: traditional history. The story describes the rift that occurs when the new chief of a tribe, Sebembele, claims as his

own the child of his late father's third junior wife. If recognized, the
child would displace Sebembele's two younger brothers in seniority. The
tribe splits in two. One camp condemns Sebembele's behavior as untra-
ditional and outrageous; the other respects his courage in standing by
his wife. The traditionalists eventually force Sebembele to leave the
kingdom with his supporters.

In outline the story is not unusual. Rivalry, secession, and tribal
migration are common enough occurrences in the histories of most
tribes and provide the background to a number of African tales. What is
significant, however, is the way Bessie Head tells the story. This is how
she sets the scene:

> Long ago, when the land was only cattle tracks and footpaths, the people
> lived together like a deep river. In this deep river which was unruffled by
> conflict or a movement forward, the people lived without faces, except
> for their chief, whose face was the face of all the people; that is, if their
> chief's name was Monemapee, then they were the people of Mon-
> emapee.[1]

The author sets up a dichotomy: there was a time when the people lived
like a deep river (a kind of prehistory before the advent of individualistic
modes of thought) and then what she calls "a movement forward" (the
modern period). While the people lived like "a deep river" there were no
individual faces; they were of one accord, and they assumed the identity
of the figurehead, their chief. The author calls this the "regimental level-
ling down of their individual souls" (*Collector*, 2). Sebembele's stand
forces the people to show their individual faces: they, as individuals,
have to decide where they stand on the issue. Are they rigidly to enforce
the time-honored laws of their forefathers, or will this provide the occasion for a major rethink?

What we have here in essence is the confrontation between old and
new, between tradition and modernity. There is a footnote to the story
that reads as follows: "The story is an entirely romanticized and fictionalized version of the history of the Botalaote tribe. Some historical data
was given to me by the old men of the tribe, but it was unreliable as
their memories had tended to fail them. A re-construction was made
therefore in my own imagination; I am also partly indebted to the London Missionary Society's '*Livingstone Tswana Readers,*' *Padiso III*, school
textbook, for those graphic paragraphs on the harvest thanksgiving ceremony which appear in the story" (*Collector*, 6).

This story clearly arose from the interviews that Head was doing for her social history, *Serowe*. She draws on the recollections of the old men of the tribe but recasts the whole story and, of course, arrives at a different conclusion from that of the old men, who say at the end that "women have always caused a lot of trouble in the world" (*Collector,* 6). What the story achieves in the context of the collection is that it sketches a mythical map of origins of the Botalaote tribe and provides a historical introduction that places the stories that follow.

The footnote to the story is highly significant: it is a candid acknowledgment of the ambiguity of the author's narrative role—her reliance on oral sources supplemented by extraneous literary ones. As we saw in the biographical outline, Head had no grounding in an African language; she was in fact schooled in English. Her background was therefore, broadly speaking, a "literate" one. She was for this reason not typical of Serowe and inevitably had a cognitive distance from all that she observed in the village. This distance she turns to her advantage in the stories: she draws on the oral texture of village life but is not compelled to adopt the majority opinion. In "The Deep River," then, we encounter a story that may originally have been told to reinforce traditional prejudices about women, but Head turns it into an occasion to celebrate the love that a tribal leader professes for one particular woman.

"Heaven Is Not Closed"

The second story retains some sort of continuity with the first in that it describes the recent history of a family and, by implication, of the community. The story opens with the author's description of the life of Galethebege, a simple yet profound woman caught between her sincere Christian convictions and Setswana custom. The authorial voice relates only the last days and death of Galethebege. The author employs the device of a storyteller, here a character in the story, the old man Modise, to tell the story of Galethebege's life:

> "I am of a mind to think that Galethebege was praying for forgiveness for her sins this morning," he said slowly. "It must have been a sin to her to marry Ralokae. He was an unbeliever to the day of his death . . .
>
> A gust of astonished laughter shook his family out of the solemn mood of mourning that had fallen upon them and they all turned eagerly towards their grandfather, sensing that he had a story to tell. (*Collector,* 8)

In a classic storytelling setting, with the "flickering firelight" lighting up their faces, the grandfather tells his family the story. The central issue is the conflict between European Christianity and Setswana custom. Galethebege wishes to get married in church. Her husband-to-be, Ralokae, is a firm traditionalist and rejects the brand of Christianity the missionaries have brought to Botswana:

> The God might be all right, he explained, but there was something wrong with the people who had brought the word of the Gospel to the land. Their love was enslaving black people and he could not stand it. . . . They had brought a new order of things into the land and they made the people cry for love. One never had to cry for love in the customary way of life. Respect was just there for people all the time. That was why he rejected all things foreign. (*Collector,* 9–10)

Galethebege's appeal to the missionary for his blessing on the marriage prompts the wry authorial comment "as though a compromise of tenderness could be made between two traditions opposed to each other" (10–11). His reply, " '[H]eaven is closed to the unbeliever' " devastates her (11). She and her family and friends all leave the church in a silent statement of protest against the attitude of the missionary.

On her deathbed, Galethebege, who had never entirely discarded her unique version of Christianity, comes to terms with her God. Her last words are: " 'I shall rest now because I believe in God' " (*Collector,* 7). Modise ends on a note that leaves his listeners to reevaluate silently the issue of the conflict between Christianity and Setswana custom: "The old man leaned forward and stirred the dying fire with a partially burnt-out log of wood. His listeners sighed the way people do when they have heard a particularly good story. As they stared at the fire they found themselves debating the matter in their minds, as their elders had done some forty or fifty years ago" (12).

"Heaven Is Not Closed" arose from an interview that appears in a chapter of *Serowe* dealing with religion in the village. The bare bones of the story are all in the interview: Segametse Mpulambusi describes her grandmother's conflict with and withdrawal from the London Missionary Society church. It was possibly the interview context that prompted the author to introduce the device of the storyteller when she retold the story in a fictive mode.

Through this device the author is able to present all the familiar components of an African storytelling ethos: the campfire setting, the old and wise narrator, a known and intimate audience, an ending that provokes reevaluation and comment. The reader is introduced to the texture of village life by being drawn to the campfire, as it were, by the storyteller's compelling technique (the storyteller here being both the character, Modise, and the authorial voice).

"Heaven Is Not Closed," in other words, is an example of how the collection as a whole is an attempt to evoke the life of a Botswanan village for the reader by reconstructing the way the village explains itself. The narrative tale, the primary method—according to Walter J. Ong[2]—by which oral cultures deal with the flow of life is therefore the genre Head adopts. The stories are the kind that the villagers tell each other. They are contained by a larger narrative framework (explicitly at work in "Heaven Is Not Closed") that contextualizes the tales for the reader and transcribes the oral tale into the written short story.

The author breaks into the narrative of "Heaven Is Not Closed." She employs the device of the storyteller to evoke the flavor of village life in a tangible way but does not restrict herself to what a person of Modise's age and context would conceivably tell. By evoking the traditional oral storyteller within the text of a modern short story, the story's structure works with a double edge to give a sense of that which it describes. The story conveys its meaning, in other words, in two ways: by what is said and by how it says it.

"Life"

A sense of historical moment—both ancient and modern—is very strong in the stories. Each story is firmly rooted in its historical particularity, and the opening passages of "Life" are a good example of this:

> In 1963, when the borders were first set up between Botswana and South Africa, pending Botswana's independence in 1966, all Botswana-born citizens had to return home. . . . On their return they brought with them bits and bits of a foreign culture and city habits which they had absorbed. Village people reacted in their own way; what they liked, and was beneficial to them—they absorbed, for instance the faith-healing cult churches which instantly took hold like wildfire—what was harmful to them, they rejected. The murder of Life had this complicated undertone of rejection. (*Collector*, 37)

The collision of two worlds is the central issue of the story. Life, a young, attractive and sexually permissive girl, returns from Johannesburg, an environment that spawned a free lifestyle, and meets and finally marries

Lesego, a representative of traditional village life and values. Before she marries, however, she becomes the village's first prostitute and operates in the local hotel bar. Life cannot shed this former way of life and slides back into it in Lesego's absence. He returns from his lands to discover this breach of fidelity and with calculated deliberateness kills her.

What is obviously at issue here is the intrusion of modern urban values into traditional village life. When one woman curiously asks Life about her seemingly endless stream of money, she gets the following response: " 'Money flows like water in Johannesburg,' Life replied, with her gay and hysterical laugh. 'You just have to know how to get it' " (*Collector,* 38). The group of women respond to this with caution: "They said among themselves that their child could not have lived a very good life in Johannesburg. Thrift and honesty were the dominant themes of village life and everyone knew that one could not be honest and rich at the same time; they counted every penny and knew how they had acquired it—with hard work. They never imagined money as a bottomless pit without end; it always had an end and was hard to come by in this dry, semi-desert land" (38–39).

It is precisely these values and this environment that eventually stifle Life and drive her to rebel. Like the beer-brewing women, however, who attempt to escape the constraints of a patriarchal culture but are nonetheless abused by the men, Life cannot escape the power of patriarchy. Lesego acts coolly and decisively to restore order and reinstate traditional values. The author clearly respects these values and comes down strongly in favor of village life. Beneath the quiet, unbroken monotony of everyday life there is a rich underlife that is the core of the villagers' existence. It lacks the superficial glitter and excitement of the environment Life is used to, but it has stability as well as an interest of its own.

The story does not have a clear resolution, however. How does the author appear to judge the matter? She treats Life sympathetically: Life *is* shallow and cheap, she *does* lead a negative, destructive lifestyle, but is her fate commensurate with her misdeeds? On the other hand, the author does not unequivocally condemn Lesego either. To the end he is portrayed as a levelheaded man, hard but just. It is worth noting, however, that the author is clearly aware of the collusion between Batswana patriarchy and the white, neocolonial justice system. The white judge responds favorably to Lesego's plea that " 'a fire seemed to fill [his] heart' " when he discovered his wife's treachery: " 'This is a crime of passion,' he said sympathetically. 'So there are extenuating circumstances. But it is still a serious crime to take a human life so I sentence you to five years imprisonment' " (*Collector,* 46). This lenient sentence is clearly meant to reflect ironically on the harsh life sentence meted out to Dikeledi Mokopi in the title story of the collection, especially when one considers the extreme provocation she endured after years of abuse.

In the end, however, no authorial judgment is imposed. Unlike the novels, which have a clear didactic purpose, the stories of *The Collector of Treasures* derive their structure from the complexities of the real world. They have a whimsical, ironic quality to them, and like episodes taken from real life, they often raise issues that elude resolution. "Life" ends on the following note: "A song by Jim Reeves was very popular at that time: *That's What Happens When Two Worlds Collide.* When they were drunk, the beer-brewing women used to sing it and start weeping. Maybe they had the last word on the whole affair" (*Collector,* 46).

"Witchcraft"

There is a tension that can be identified in Head's work: her insider's understanding and yet her cultural distance, her desire to be a story-teller in the traditional mold and yet her superior knowledge of literary technique. This tension is a productive one. It gives her stories their earthy, real-life quality while providing the distance and detachment necessary for artistic creativity.

A pattern is established in Head's stories in which she introduces a typical aspect of Botswanan village life and follows it with an exemplary story that invariably deals with the life of a particular member of the community. "Witchcraft" is structured like this: it introduces the phe-nomenon and analyzes its social causes and the powerful effect it has on the lives of the people. It then goes on to tell the story of Mma-Mabele, a woman who faces the paradox of the efficacy of witchcraft in a society that is supposedly Christian and rational. Characteristically, the author offers a lot of detail about Botswanan life in the process of describing Mma-Mabele's background:

> Mma-Mabele belonged to that section of the village who rationalised quite clearly: "I know I can be poisoned and so meet my end, but I can-not be bewitched. I don't believe in it." They were the offspring of fami-lies who had deeply embraced Christianity and who were regular church-goers; when the hospital opened in the village, they had all their ailments attended to there and did not need to consult the Tswana doctor. All this provided some mental leverage to sort out the true from the false in the

everyday round of village life, but not immunity to strange forms of
assault. (*Collector,* 48)

Mma-Mabele and her sister each have an illegitimate child, and they
struggle to make enough money to keep themselves alive. (Mma-
Mabele is unable to plow the land she inherited from her parents, and it
now lies fallow.) Their fortune changes: Mma-Mabele finds a job as a
housekeeper and the monthly income of the household increases dra-
matically. She is soon a victim of jealousy, however. A patch of her hair is
mysteriously shaven one night: "In village lore, it was only one thing
that could have touched her life—the baloi" (*Collector,* 51).

From this point on, Mma-Mabele's Christian upbringing and common sense are in conflict with ancient superstition. She is approached
by Lekena, a traditional doctor, who offers his services to her. Mma-
Mabele has been able to analyze why Tswana doctors like Lekena are
sometimes able to cure and sometimes not: they "cure" bites from non-
venomous snakes and scorpions but not those from poisonous ones. Yet
she is unable to rationalize the cutout patch of her hair. She starts ailing
physically and suffers excruciating pains in the head. She then goes to
the hospital and is advised to supplement her poor diet by eating
oranges. Lekena responds to the hospital's diagnosis in the following
way: " 'They don't know everything Mma-Mabele. I told you your trouble comes from Tswana custom and I can help you too' " (*Collector,* 54).

Medicine and religion, two distinct practices in Western culture,
become a combined force in traditional Tswana custom and pose a challenge to Mma-Mabele as a Christian convert who also believes in the
efficacy of Western medicine. She is able to rationalize the practice of
witchcraft but is not able to reason away the demons that are afflicting
her. Ultimately, however, through common sense and sheer determination she is able to regain her health. Her concluding retort to her friends
clearly carries the author's approbation: " 'You all make me sick! There
is no one to help the people, not even God. I could not sit down because
I am too poor and there is no one else to feed my children' " (*Collector,*
56). Daily exigencies force aside the esoteric dabblings of witchcraft, and
the ending serves as an affirmation of human courage in the face of
adversity.

Yet the story as a whole is ambiguous. Mma-Mabele's rejection of
witchcraft does not enable her to escape it. Witchcraft is shown to be at
once a sham as well as effective; it is fraudulent and yet wields real
power in the society. This ambiguity appears to arise from the author's

own uncertainties. As a city-bred outsider, brought up outside the ambit of the supernatural, she responds with skepticism and yet is unwilling to spurn entirely the power of witchcraft. A comment that occurs at the beginning of the story expresses her attitude to the phenomenon: "One cannot help but conclude that if a whole society creates a belief in something, that something is likely to become real" (*Collector,* 47).

"Kgotla"

If there is a single theme binding the stories together, it is that of modernity intruding into the world of tradition. Each of the stories explores a different facet of the inexorable movement of traditional Batswana culture into the modern era. Three stories deal with this theme most explicitly. "Life," as we saw, examines the clash between traditional village culture and values and the lifestyle brought back from the urban, moneyed Johannesburg metropolis. "The Wind and a Boy" explores the recklessness and tragedy engendered by the tensions of a society in transition. "Kgotla" (meaning "tribal court" in Setswana) deals with the internal changes in Botswana in the political realm, where tribal tradition encounters modern, postindependent administration.

In "Kgotla" the old and the new Botswana are juxtaposed:

> Behind the kgotla, an administrative block had been set up to modernize village life. It fussed about schools, boreholes, roads, development, and progress; energetic young clerks dashed from one department to another, their hands filled with bureaucratic paperwork. They had no time to listen to the twitter of birds in the ancient shady trees that surrounded the kgotla, but the two worlds daily travelled side by side and the bureaucratic world was fast devouring up the activities of the ancient, rambling kgotla world. (*Collector,* 61–62)

What is at issue in the story is the opposed sets of values embodied by the kgotla and the new administrative block respectively. The story skillfully presents the physical intrusion of the new into the old and the psychological changes this produces. The leisurely, time-honored, dignified world of the kgotla is seen to be in greater harmony with Botswanan life than the new administrators, who "fussed" about schools, boreholes, and the like. The kgotla is also described as the "people's place" where they could make "their anguish and disputes heard" (62). It has as its basis human nature and incorporates this into its body of law: "There, at the kgotla, it wasn't so important to resolve human problems as to discuss around them, to pontificate, to generalize, to display wit, wisdom, wealth of experience or depth of thought. All this made the kgotla world a holy world that moved at its own pace and time" (62).

The contrast here is between modern efficiency and a scientific approach to problems, on the one hand, and time-honored wisdom, wit, and understanding on the other. As the case of the day illustrates, however, the kgotla has its own kind of efficiency. The case is a domestic dispute between a man's lawful wife and his mistress. The man at the center of the dispute is unable to pay back the R300 that his mistress brought into the household. She demands the return of the money before she relinquishes her position to the lawful wife. The court founders momentarily; however, the education that the wife has received makes a resolution possible: she is able to find a job and pay back the money.

The story is significant because it reveals Head's views on independence and change in Botswana. Independence has brought a new, efficient bureaucracy with it, yet it has lost touch with the world of the kgotla, which preserves an essentially humanistic orientation. Education and the availability of jobs facilitate solutions to hitherto insurmountable problems, yet they hasten the erosion of an older, more graceful and harmonious world.

"The Wind and a Boy"

The short story has qualities that make it a highly appropriate medium for the expression of communal experience. Its brevity approximates the episodic quality of everyday life. And as episodes from daily life, short stories can deal separately with different subjectivities, thereby intensifying the individual focus of each story. A collection of stories like *The Collector of Treasures* is thus a composite portrait of a total world: it builds up the complete picture by dealing piecemeal with fragments of the whole. Each story can overlap with the next or imply the presence of the next without losing intensity. Head contains in each story a moment from the lives of the people involved. The collection is an aggregate of these moments, constituting, in total, a portrait of Serowe village.

This explains the special ability the stories of *The Collector of Treasures* have for giving representative rather than unique examples of village life. Each of the stories describes a particular episode, and yet each also is typical of village life. The opening passages of "The Wind and a Boy" illustrate this quality: "Until they became ordinary, dull grown men, who drank beer and made babies, the little village boys were a special set all on their own. They were kings whom no one ruled" (*Collector,* 69).

The story describes how the little boys go hunting when the first hard rains of summer fall. Wild rabbits, moles, and porcupines would be drowned in their burrows. The little boys have a characteristic response to this: "As they pulled out the animal, they would say, pityingly: 'Birds have more sense than rabbits, moles and porcupines. They build their homes in trees' " (*Collector,* 69).

These extracts demonstrate Head's concern to portray village life by describing what is general and characteristic of the village. This is one of the ways in which the close unity of the stories and the complete portrait they constitute is achieved. Another is the way Head firmly places the stories in their historical moment. The passage of time, and the change wrought by this historical process, is the context in which all the stories are set and from which they derive their meaning. Almost all of the stories have details that locate them at a point in Botswana's historical development. For instance, until the closing passages, the story of Friedman and his grandmother ("The Wind and a Boy") appears to be an entirely personal, individualized portrait of a unique relationship. And indeed, this is certainly an important dimension of the story. But Head is not simply content to leave it at that; she does not conclude the story without providing the underlying historical moment that ultimately gives it its wider social resonance.

Friedman's advent, to begin with, is an illustration of the unhappy state of family life, the economic pressures exerted on women in the postindependent period, and relations between the Batswana and foreign-aid workers:

> All Sejosenye's children were grown, married, and had left home. Of all her children, only her last-born daughter was unmarried and Friedman was the result of some casual mating she had indulged in, in a town a hundred miles away where she had a job as a typist. She wanted to return to her job almost immediately, so she handed the child over to her mother and that was that; she could afford to forget him as he had a real mother now. During all the time that Sejosenye haunted the hospital, awaiting her bundle, a friendly foreign doctor named Friedman took a fancy to her maternal, grandmotherly ways. He made a habit of walking out of his path to talk to her. She never forgot it and on receiving her bundle she called the baby, Friedman. (*Collector,* 70)

In a single paragraph, Head deftly renders a host of details about contemporary life in Botswana. It is Botswana at a particular phase in its development: new job opportunities are being offered to hitherto domesticated, traditional women; new administrative and industrial towns are springing up, and the breakdown of family life and the consequent vulnerability of women is becoming widespread.

The story describes Friedman's boyhood and poignantly depicts the growing affection between him and his grandmother. Tragedy occurs when Friedman reaches the age of 14 and acquires a bicycle with which to run errands for his grandmother. On a trip back from their lands to town to buy provisions, Friedman is killed in a collision with a truck. His grandmother loses her mind and dies two weeks later. The story concludes in this way:

> As was village habit, the incident was discussed thoroughly from all sides till it was understood. In this timeless, sleepy village, the goats stood and suckled their young ones on the main road or lay down and took their afternoon naps there. The motorists either stopped for them or gave way. But it appeared that the driver of the truck had neither brakes on his car nor a driving licence. He belonged to the new, rich civil-servant class whose salaries had become fantastically high since independence. They had to have cars in keeping with their new status; they had to have any car, as long as it was a car; they were in such a hurry about everything that they couldn't be bothered to take driving lessons. And thus progress, development, and a pre-occupation with status and living-standards first announced themselves to the village. It looked like being an ugly story with many decapitated bodies on the main road. (*Collector*, 75)

There is a literal and metaphorical collision here between old and new. The tale of a little boy and his grandmother is thus presented with a strong sociopolitical underpinning, and the tragedy is both a personal and a social one. The story of Friedman and his grandmother is typical of the collection: it is a highly individualized story about a beautiful boy and his relationship with his grandmother. Yet it assumes a sociohistorical significance in the moral question that emerges at the end: what do modernity and independence hold in store for the ordinary villager?

The stories of *The Collector of Treasures* make it clear that individual experience—the private lives the author explores—is meant to communicate or exemplify the collective experience of the community. The moral impetus for this is Head's conviction that the individual is important but that in an ideal sharing community, the personal is not stressed in opposition to collective experience. Private experience is no longer to be hoarded against the lean days of individual alienation. It is with a stoical sense of the primacy of the personal core that she writes her novels. Her later sense of belonging and commitment makes possible an affirmation of communal experience that is at the heart of the stories of *The Collector of Treasures*.

"The Collector of Treasures"

It was suggested at the beginning of this chapter that the stories of *The Collector of Treasures* bear an interesting relation to Botswanan oral culture. Head shows considerable interest in the figure of the storyteller, who has a prominent role in the village life of which she was a part. *Serowe* abounds in descriptions of the old and wise men whom other villagers proudly refer to as "our traditional historians." In *The Collector of Treasures,* the title story sheds light on her conception of the storyteller.

The story arose in what Head called "village newspaper" fashion from an encounter she had with a relative of the man who was killed by his estranged wife.[3] As with "Heaven Is Not Closed," she leaves the story line intact. When she retells the story, however, she supplies an analysis of the social breakdown occurring in modern Botswanan society and the kinds of problems to which this gives rise: "There were really only two kinds of men in the society. The one kind created such misery and chaos that he could be broadly damned as evil. . . . Since that kind of man was in the majority in the society, he needed a little analysing as he was responsible for the complete breakdown of family life" (*Collector,* 91).

She goes on to analyze the fate of this kind of man over three time spans: the tribal period, the colonial period, and the period of independence. The first robbed him of individuality and the ability to think independently. The second turned him into a migrant laborer and broke the traditional form of family life. Independence then changed this pattern: "More jobs became available under the new government's localization programme and salaries sky-rocketed at the same time. It provided the first occasion for family life of a new order, above the childlike discipline of custom, the degradation of colonialism. Men and women, in order to survive, had to turn inwards to their own resources. It was the man who arrived at this turning point, a broken wreck with no inner resources at all" (*Collector,* 92).

In the greater context of migrant labor, city life, and the breakdown of the family, the personal tragedy of Dikeledi occurs. She is deserted by her husband, Garesego, who leaves her to fend for herself and their three children while he pursues other women. With considerable resourcefulness she manages to support herself and her children and to bring her life to a point where it becomes "holy" to her (*Collector*, 101). Her new neighbors are exemplars of a modern, progressive, happy Botswanan family, and she shares in their happiness. This pattern is broken when she is forced to approach her husband for money to send their eldest son to secondary school. Garesego is bitterly jealous of the life Dikeledi shares with her neighbors and decides to return for a night to reestablish his territory. Dikeledi sees no way out of the problem: she kills her husband by castrating him and is jailed for life.

Her tragedy is not unique. In prison she shares a cell with four other women who have killed their husbands. As the wardress sardonically remarks: " 'It's becoming the fashion these days' " (*Collector*, 88). There is a distinct sense in the story that society is punishing the victims, not the offenders. Together the victims try to reconstruct a life for themselves: "And so the woman Dikeledi began phase three of a life that had been ashen in its loneliness and unhappiness. And yet she had always found gold amidst the ash, deep loves that had joined her heart to the hearts of others. She smiled tenderly at Kebonye because she knew already that she had found another such love. She was the collector of such treasures" (91).

There are some remarkable features to the story. In the first place, Head is taking up a feminist cause in a society distinctly hostile to this phenomenon. She places the story in a specific sociohistorical context and thereby *politicizes* Dikeledi's dilemma. By refusing to sensationalize the incident and by insisting that Dikeledi's act should not be seen as an arbitrary act of retribution but as a socially determined act she is making a political statement.

At another level of interpretation what Head attempts in "The Collector of Treasures" is to resolve contradictory forces in Botswanan society via the character Paul Thebolo. He is an example of what she calls the "kind of man in the society with the power to create himself anew" (*Collector*, 93). That she chooses a man is significant: in a society that is, by her own witness, crippled by an a priori assumption of male superiority, she cannot conceptualize beyond the male principal, the traditional head of society.

The author's attempt formally to resolve social contradictions yields textual peculiarities. In the title story, the "saviour-figures" (Paul Thebolo and the women of the prison) are rendered symbolically, which is at variance with the strong social-realist grounding of the antagonists. This is how Head described Paul Thebolo in an interview: "One of the examples where I deliberately use the problem-solving man is in the collection of short stories. There is this *majestic* man in "The Collector of Treasures"—Paul Thebolo. Now, he's juxtaposed against a man who has low animal tendencies" (*Between the Lines,* 13).

The story, as I have already noted, was prompted by a real incident that was related to the author by relatives of the man killed. Head responds to the story, which she says profoundly shocked her, by proposing a solution. Her solution, however, is not grounded in social reality. Thebolo is idealized; he is not shown to have been shaped by society the way Garesego has been. The characterization of Thebolo and Dikeledi's cell mates therefore appear as "quirks" in the text, peculiarities superadded to the episode drawn from village life. The power to redeem society is vested in idealized savior figures, and the thorough historical understanding that underpins the stories is suspended when a solution is imposed.

This incongruity—the mixture of realism and idealism—is a function of the author's deep concern for the future of the community she describes, but unlike other African writers who romanticize the past, Head looks to the future for new ways of coping with present problems. Her stories have their unusual shape precisely because they attempt to offer new alternatives for the creation of a better society. They draw on the tragedies, mishaps, and problems of village life but are not content simply to dwell on misfortune. In "The Collector of Treasures" Head alters a real-life story to incorporate a proposed solution: a man who can cope with change and offer modern Botswana an alternative to family breakdown and the destruction of the social order.

The title story holds the key to the way the collection works. The crucial thrust of the story is the creation of beauty, of happiness, of human compassion and understanding in a society that is in a state of upheaval. This was the center of Head's concerns in her own life, and it is the moral impetus for her writing. Dikeledi is the collector of treasures. The author was also the collector of treasures, of which Dikeledi's story is one. The book is a collection of treasures, of finely crafted stories, that offer the reader exemplary tales of resilience, compassion, and human understanding. The intention, in short, is to discover and refine "gold amidst the ash" (*Collector,* 91).

"Hunting"

The German theorist Walter Benjamin had the following to say about the novel and how it differs from storytelling: "What differentiates the novel from all other forms of prose literature—the fairy tale, the legend, even the novella—is that it neither comes from oral tradition nor goes into it. This distinguishes it from storytelling in particular. . . . The novelist has isolated himself. The birthplace of the novel is the solitary individual, who is no longer able to express himself by giving examples of his most important concerns, is himself uncounseled, and cannot counsel others."[4]

If the solitary individual is the birthplace of the novel, then community is the birthplace of the story. Stories told imply listeners, and this is nowhere more evident than in the community of the village. In his *Pig Earth,* John Berger makes this observation: "All villages tell stories. Stories of the past, even of the distant past. . . . And, equally, stories of the very same day. Most of what happens during a day is recounted by somebody before the day ends. The stories are factual, based on observation or on a first-hand account. This combination of the sharpest observation, of the daily recounting of the day's events and encounters, and of lifelong mutual familiarities is what constitutes so-called village *gossip*" (Berger, 8).

The story "Hunting" is set in just such a milieu. It concerns the relationship between a man and his wife, and their relationship with the rest of the village. It is hunting season in the village, and four men keep "an anxious watch on the yard of the man, Tholo" (*Collector,* 104). They hope to ride on his tractor when they go hunting, which would allow them to spend minimum time roughing it in the bush and would eliminate the arduous journey by foot. Tholo's quiet self-assurance and inherent goodness are exemplary and do not escape the attention of the village: "That was what every man knew about Tholo—that he was a good man. He never refused a request for help and shared generously all he had with others. But beyond that the man in him seemed to run away from all the conflicts of life. There was no order or goodness in human life, but there was an order and soundness in everything he could control or communicate with. He communicated deeply, with his wife, and his work" (105).

It is this exemplary relationship between a man and his wife that is at the center of the story. We learn that Tholo married Thato when she already had a child by another man who had deserted her, "a common experience for most women these days" (*Collector,* 105). The abuse of women—a theme that runs through the entire collection of stories—is brought sharply to the fore here. Thato first encounters Tholo when he comes to plow the family's land, and he makes a strong impression on the young girl: "By night, an unmoving image had haunted her dreams of a man's head turned sideways in fixed concentration as he closely watched the contours and furrows he created behind him. She had cried a little to herself; he had seemed a creature too far removed from her own humble life" (106). They meet again and start a relationship. Then Thato becomes pregnant, and she goes into a state of depression: she loves Tholo but knows that when she tells him that she is pregnant he will desert her, as the other man did. His response is unexpected: " 'We can get married,' he said softly. 'I can arrange everything' " (107). The character of this unusual man is summed up in one sentence: "He was incapable of hurting life. . . . [B]asically he cared about everything" (107).

Thato herself brings a special quality to the relationship. At the end of each day she would recount the day's events to her husband: "She had the capacity to live with the conflicts of life in a way he had not. Like all women, she was involved in village gossip and disputes. She knew everything, but the richness of her communication lay in her gift to sift and sort out all the calamities of everyday life with the unerring heart of a good storyteller" (*Collector,* 108–9). From his wife Tholo knows that Rapula, one of the men who came to see him earlier, has taken up with a shebeen queen and beat his wife when she remonstrated with him. The story ends on a wry, ambivalent note: "What could be done? Nothing could sort out the world. It would always be a painful muddle. That was why he had turned to Rapula and smiled like God, in a kind and friendly way" (109).

So Thato tells stories. Using the storyteller's craft of sifting and sorting, she describes events she has seen or about which she has heard. Other villagers are possibly describing her in this way. Taken all together, these stories constitute what Berger calls the "village's portrait of itself." The function of "close, oral, daily history," he argues, "is to allow the whole village to define itself" (Berger, 9).

It is this source that Bessie Head taps in producing *The Collector of Treasures.* She transcribes oral sources into literature and reshapes the spoken to suit the new medium of the written, the guiding intention being to explain a village in its own terms. Deeply sympathetic and understanding, and at the same time possessing an astute ability to analyze, she is able, as Berger puts it, to "see how events fits together" (Berger, 12).

Chapter Nine
Serowe: Village of the Rain Wind (1981)

Serowe: Village of the Rain Wind can be seen in many ways as a documentary companion to *The Collector of Treasures*. Whereas the stories are an attempt to render the life of the village filtered through the author's imagination, the social history is an attempt to allow the villagers to speak for themselves. So although *The Collector of Treasures* clearly draws its subject matter from the life of Serowe village, the final shape and moral direction the stories are given are of the author's making. *Serowe* is a more complex undertaking. There is a critical, and often indistinguishable, mixture of an interview participant's contribution and authorial intervention. How much of *Serowe* is of the author's design and how much is dictated by the villagers, whose interviews are after all intended to represent the voice of Serowe? This is one of the critical questions *Serowe* elicits.

The book is composed of a series of transcribed interviews edited and prefaced to constitute a portrait of Serowe village. The primary historians in this case are the people themselves. The author introduces the village by general description, and the interview material is then shaped and arranged into historical and thematic groupings. In her introduction Head describes the book in this way: "The book is built around the lives and work of three men—Khama the Great, Tshekedi Khama, and Patrick van Rensburg—and the story of Serowe is told through their contributions to the community and the response of that community to their ideals and ideas."[1] She concludes by observing: "I shall attempt to tie three great personalities together and around their lives and work, draw a portrait of Serowe."

The three sections of the book—which comprise the eras of Khama the Great, Tshekedi Khama, and Patrick van Rensburg—each contain details that illustrate the specific periods they cover as well as themes that portray the historical continuity and development of the Bamangwato people. Clearly Head was concerned with the particular characteristics of a people at various stages in their development as well as with the continuity in this development.

The first section deals with issues that characterize Khama the Great's era: the man's stature, his struggles with his father, the reforms he introduced, the introduction of Christianity into traditional society, the evolution of African "faith-healing churches," and the nature of society at the time of the advent of the white traders. Especially characteristic of Khama's era was the role of the old men in transmitting traditional history. The memories and tales of an old traditional historian, Mokgojwa Mathware, for instance, form a vague, near-mythical background to the history of the Bamangwato people. Head comments: "He can tell you endless tales about the long, dim past, which is a pain to no one, but nothing about the near present, which is a pain to everyone" (*Serowe*, 11).

The "long, dim past" is of interest to Head only in that it provides insights into the "near present," with which she is more immediately engaged. The old man's narratives nonetheless provide a sense of origins, not only of his society but also of the way in which that society expresses itself: "I did not attend school. At the cattle-post we lived with older men, and in the evenings we sat around the fire and listened to the older men talking. That was when I learnt about the history of my tribe. They talked about the past of the Bamangwato; their chiefs and the battles they fought with other tribes. I have remembered every word to this day" (*Serowe*, 12).

The ancient oral tradition of the Bamangwato people is evoked here. The old man tells tales of tribal history, two of which Head presents in the text. They create a quasi-mythological tone that fades, as the past fades, when the interviews become more concerned with recent history and concrete events. This is one of the many ways in which the narrative structure of the text parallels that which Head constructs in *The Collector of Treasures*.

The centrality of the chief's kgotla in the lives of the Serowe villagers is another typical aspect of Khama's era. Head notes that the chief's kgotla administered more than just the everyday affairs of the people: "It was more than an administrative centre—the older people say the kgotla was the central part of their moral life, the sort of moral centre that was only paralleled by the instruction of the Christian church" (*Serowe*, 37). Khama epitomized the old order: he was in every way a competent ruler, and the future of the Bamangwato tribe would owe a lot to his wise government. Head's admiration for the man is clear: "The Bamangwato had the good fortune to be governed by a sage" (38).

Tshekedi Khama's time, Head observes at the beginning of part 2 of *Serowe*, "was famed for educational progress, and the ideal of self-help was introduced into Serowe life long before it became an international byword or necessity" (77). Tshekedi (Khama the Great's son) continued his father's wise governance: under his administration a number of schools, among them Moeng College, were built in Serowe. This was achieved through the use of work regiments: the community called on young men of a particular age regiment to offer voluntary and unpaid labor. It was on this spirit of self-help and community service that Patrick van Rensburg could later draw, and it is this spirit that Head tries to reinvoke in the testimonies of Serowans.

Self-help, education, regiment labor, the role of the white traders, and the clash between traditional and modern medicine are themes that are explored in part 2 of *Serowe*. The following example illustrates Head's approach to a particular theme. In an interview with a personal friend, Head demonstrates her concern with describing and understanding people in their social context. Her description of her friend Tlhoka-Ina simultaneously offers a portrait of the society at large: "Traditional African life has its mean individuals and its good individuals—the mean are often embarrassed into a display of generosity; the good, and Tlhoka-Ina is one of them, are simply a direct expression of all that is to be most treasured in the 'law' or traditional custom. . . . All that was naturally beautiful in the society was sharpened and given direction by men such as Tshekedi Khama, and Tlhoka-Ina grew up during the Tshekedi era" (*Serowe*, 83).

Tlhoka-Ina provides a vivid picture of the educational fervor during Tshekedi's time: "At that time, schooling ended with primary education in Serowe. For further education most of us had to take the train to South Africa. . . . We all had to assemble at the kgotla and Chief Tshekedi provided free transport for us to Palapye station and on our return, free transport back to Serowe. . . . It was never consciously in our minds and yet, being given free transport did create in us a sense of indebtedness to come back and help our people" (*Serowe*, 85).

Regimental labor ran alongside educational progress. Tshekedi drew on the ancient tradition of age regiments that had been reformed during Khama's rule. Khama had removed the ritual and secrecy surrounding the initiation ceremony and had put the regiments to constructive tasks. Tshekedi exacted enormous amounts of voluntary labor from the regiments: schools were built, dams, fences, and roads constructed, and land cleared.

Tshekedi was forced into exile when the dispute about tribal leadership began with Seretse Khama, his nephew. Tshekedi was acting as regent until the young Seretse, heir to the Bamangwato chieftaincy, came of age. When Seretse married Ruth Williams, an Englishwoman he met when studying law at Oxford, he split the tribe in two. Some were for accepting the marriage and securing a leader; the others, under Tshekedi, rejected the marriage altogether. The second group moved with Tshekedi in 1952 to establish Pilikwe village, some 80 kilometers away from Serowe. Head comments on this move as follows:

> The families who made the big move with Tshekedi all belonged to the upper crust of Serowe society and this detail alone is an indication of the quality of African society. When men, who are rich, secure and in key positions in a society, break up their homes and jobs overnight to face the unknown, homeless—their motivations bear examining. This historical story was the last of the migrations in the old African tradition—a tradition established over the centuries to avert bloodshed in a crisis and underlying the basic non-violent nature of African society as it was then. This gives the lie to white historians who, for their own ends, damned African people as savages. (*Serowe*, 95)

This passage makes it clear that Head wished to restore balance to the historical record; indeed, *Serowe* as a whole attempts to do this by reinterpreting from a fresh perspective the key events of Bamangwato history. One of those who moved with Tshekedi, a schoolteacher, gives his judgment on the matter: "It was not a question of loving power or position, which we all had. It was a question of moving off with a man we could not do without. It takes a man years to build his home, so you can see what it cost us. That is our history and that is the way our history always turned out" (98).

This history, as we saw, found its way into Head's fictional work as well. The opening story of *The Collector of Treasures* deals with just such a tribal schism—this time a very ancient, almost forgotten one, when the Botalaote tribe lived farther north in Africa. Again, Head's source is her interviews, although her informants in this case were so unreliable that she was forced to abandon plans to include their testimony in *Serowe* and to present it as "an entirely romanticized and fictionalized version" in her companion collection of stories (*Collector*, 6). Earlier, in *Maru*, we saw an echo of this pattern of peaceful tribal schism when Maru, like

Tshekedi Khama, moves away from his tribe in the wake of the contro-versy of his marriage to the "Masarwa" woman Margaret.

Head begins the third part of *Serowe* with an appraisal of Patrick van Rensburg's personality and achievements: "He has an air of impersonal abstraction, the legend and the fame. The legend was his diplomatic position in South Africa and his abdication from that position on moral grounds. In later years the fame of his educational theories for develop-ing countries spread far and wide" (*Serowe,* 135).

Head clearly discerns Van Rensburg's continuity with the past. He came to a part of Africa ready to answer his call to self-help: "Perhaps he already knew of the older generation who had helped build the primary schools of Serowe with voluntary labour in Tshekedi's time, and that their offspring would understand a call to service" (136). Van Rensburg initi-ated the "Swaneng Project," which was the construction and administer-ing of a secondary school a few kilometers outside Serowe. A passage from *Serowe* describes the spirit of the venture and how it was made possi-ble: "Initially teachers would teach with only one wall of a classroom con-structed, and at weekends both teachers and students would join forces to continue the building of the school. Finance came from aid money and further building was done through organized work camps" (136).

Self-sufficiency and progress of this nature are ideals to which Head passionately adhered; they parallel her own struggle to take root. Hence her spirited description of the Farmers' Brigade, one of the brigades Van Rensburg adapted from the age-regiment system: "Each day, early in the morning, the milk cart of the Serowe Farmers' Brigade wends its way through the dusty tracks and pathways of Serowe. At a shout from the young lads and the clank of the milk cans, housewives on the route hurry outdoors with their jugs to collect their daily supply of fresh milk, eggs, cheese and vegetables. Although today, the milk-cart is a familiar part of the Serowe scene, such farming produce was an undreamed-of wonder a few years ago" (*Serowe,* 147). The brigades put into practice Head's desire to create "new worlds out of nothing" (*Woman Alone,* 28). Their success in wresting produce from the barren soil of Botswana had a special meaning for Head, whose own creativity can be seen as an analogous activity.

The remarkable aspect of the self-help projects of Van Rensburg and of his predecessors Khama and Tshekedi Khama is the willingness, as the author reveals, of the villagers—who had had a protracted history of struggling to subsist—to support new, revolutionary schemes. *Serowe* unfolds the significant change in the orientation of society that began with Khama and his reforms. The Christianization of Batswana custom and the reform of many traditional practices under Khama amounted to nothing less than a transformation of the society. The initiation ceremonies for men and women and *bogadi,* the bride price for women, were cornerstones of Tswana custom. Their redirection or removal indicates both the strength of Khama's leadership and the people's willingness to change. That Khama was able to use voluntary labor for community projects indicates also the people's readiness to share and to help each other. Tshekedi Khama exacted more demanding forms of unpaid labor to build necessities like schools, hospitals, and roads. For his part, Patrick van Rensburg built on the innate progressiveness of the Bamangwato people to experiment with new ways of subsisting and with other novel schemes: a school with a self-help program, self-supporting training schemes, cooperative shops, and cooperative projects of all kinds.

Boiteko, which the author roughly translates as "many hands make light work" (*Serowe,* 170), is an example of these cooperative projects. Head offers a keen insight into the effects of their newly learned skills on the ordinary people participating in *Boiteko:* "Like all the other projects, new skills and new ideas invade people's lives. The poor and illiterate are slowly building up their own economy where no one is exploiting them and they control their own affairs. It is a common sight at *Boiteko* to see a member pick up a garment or an article and say, with a very learned air: 'Now what are my production costs? How am I going to price this article?' " (*Serowe,* 172). The book is accented by poignant impressions like this: it is a feature of *Serowe* that makes the book highly readable while providing vivid images of village people.

As this overview perhaps suggests, Head's history of Serowe is a complex undertaking. It eschews a socioscientific approach in favor of a more creative impulse, which the author candidly acknowledges at the outset: "I chose the main theme of the book myself—that of social reform and educational progress" (*Serowe,* xv). So *Serowe* is deliberately structured to give a sense of historical continuity and social change. Authorial intervention is not an unfortunate inevitability but a guiding principle, and the author sees the interviews as material that she must put to her own artistic purpose: "It is the underlying achievement of community service which I have attempted to re-invoke from some Serowans' testimony" (77).

Head's sympathy for ordinary people and her respect for their wisdom, understanding, and way of life are never allowed to become mere liberal sentiment. Her own experience of the patronizing way whites treated blacks in South Africa prompts a more honest and immediate engagement with the Serowe villagers whose lifestyle, after all, she partly shared. This was the basis of her disagreement with Penguin, the proposed publishers, who, she argued, wanted an account of "what people ate, when they sleep, how they dress."[2] She was unwilling to supply romantic visions of, in her own words, "noble savages in skins and beads cavorting around in primitive and exotic innocence" (De Smidt, 101). Whatever the exact nature of the disagreement between Head and Penguin, she clearly felt she had a more partisan role to play. Her work is not a report back to civilization about the mysteries of "darkest Africa." It is a tribute to her village of exile, the repayment of a debt by giving the village of Serowe a voice.

Appropriately enough, Ronald Blythe, author of *Akenfield* (which provided some kind of model to Head in the early stages of her own book), wrote the foreword to *Serowe*. Its opening passage reads: "I felt as I came to the end of this unforgettable book that I had understood not only Serowe, the huge Botswanan village which Bessie Head describes, but for the first time certain things about Africa itself which had never before found their way into literature. A new light floods in on the scene when, early on, she quietly states that Africa was never 'the Dark Continent' to African people" (*Serowe*, v).

The degree of the shift in perspective from her third novel, *A Question of Power*, to this position, which Blythe so astutely registers, gives an idea of Head's quiet but dramatic affirmation of her new home in *Serowe*. She repeats part of a passage from the early, eulogistic piece "For Serowe: A Village in Africa" (1965) in her introduction to *Serowe*: "It was by chance that I came to live in this village. I have lived most of my life in shattered little bits. Somehow, here, the shattered bits began to grow together. There is a sense of wovenness, a wholeness in life here; a feeling of how strange and beautiful people can be—just living" (x).

The book ends with an epilogue, which Head calls a "poem to Serowe" (*Serowe*, 179). It is worth repeating in full, as it gives a rich sense of the author's feeling of both possessing and being possessed:

These I have loved:
The hours I spent collecting together my birds, my pathways, my sunsets, and shared them, with everyone; The small boys of this village and their homemade wire cars; The windy nights, when the vast land mass outside my door simulates the dark roar of the ocean.

—And those mysteries: that one bird call at dawn—that single, solitary outdoor fireplace far in the bush that always captivates my eye. Who lives so far away in the middle of nowhere? The wedding parties and beer parties of my next-door neighbours that startle with their vigour and rowdiness; The very old women of the village who know so well how to plough with a hoe; their friendly motherliness and insistent greetings as they pass my fence with loads of firewood or water buckets on their heads; My home at night and the hours I spent outside it watching the yellow glow of the candle-light through the curtains; The hours I spent inside it in long, solitary thought.

These small joys were all I had, with nothing beyond them, they were indulged in over and over again, like my favourite books. (*Serowe,* 179)

Serowe includes an appendix on the founding of the Bechuanaland Protectorate. Head was clearly fascinated by Botswana's unusual history, and the appendix reveals her considerable skill in assimilating and synthesizing this historical material. The emphasis is ultimately on the uniqueness of Botswana in southern African history and on the role of Khama the Great in this historical process.

Head also notes the irony in modern Botswana's debt to the failed Jameson Raid: "The failure of the Jameson Raid confirmed the independent existence of the British Bechuanaland Protectorate under direct rule from London. In 1966 it became the independent state of Botswana. Botswana has experienced a history without parallel in southern Africa. If the indigenous people had lost their lands, they would have lost everything and become slaves and a source of cheap labour to any white exploiter at hand" (*Serowe,* 198).

It is an incongruous mixture of chance and skillful diplomacy that contributes to the magic of Botswana, which Head notices throughout and renders in her work. *Serowe* captures the magic of her village in Botswana without forfeiting a sense of the reality of its hardships and its struggle to survive.

Chapter Ten
A Bewitched Crossroad (1984)

A Bewitched Crossroad: An African Saga again shows Head attempting a synthesis of fictional and documentary discourses.[1] For this reason it can be seen as having developed directly from the preoccupations of its predecessor, *Serowe: Village of the Rain Wind.* The text attempts two things simultaneously: it describes the process of establishing the British Protectorate of Bechuanaland, and it tells the story of Sebina, the leader of a clan that is eventually absorbed into the Bamangwato nation under Khama the Great.

The story begins circa 1800, when the Sebina clan under Motswaing separated from the Barolong tribe and migrated northward, eventually joining with other immigrant clans under Mambo, a king in the legendary Mwene-Mutapa dynasty. By the time this occurs Motswaing has died, and it is his son, Sebina, who secures a permanent abode for the clan. Peace is disrupted when the warlike Matabele, under their famous chief Mzilikazi, attack the settlement.

The Matabele have themselves been displaced from their original home in Natal, and the narrative digresses at this point to fill in the historical background of the "Wars of Calamity" of the early 1800s, a dramatic period of upheaval in southern Africa better known as the Mfecane. Head briefly sketches the rise of Shaka, king of the Zulus, and describes the widespread depredations caused in the southern African hinterland by his drive to establish a military empire. Smaller tribes that had hitherto lived alongside each other in peace found themselves the victims of Shaka's raids and turned on each other to secure land and a means of existence. Out of this situation of chaos and bloodshed emerged such nation-building leaders as Moshoeshoe, who gathered displaced tribes together at his mountain stronghold of Thaba Bosigo.

Another digression from the main narrative occurs at this point as Head sketches the background of European settlement of South Africa, from the Dutch colonization in the mid-seventeenth century to British intervention in the early 1800s. One important consequence of the conflict between Dutch settlers and the British colonial administration was the Great Trek of 1836, which threw the southern African hinterland into even greater chaos and disruption. The mineral discoveries of the late nineteenth century then gave even greater impetus to the European drive to acquire land, and the black tribes in the Transvaal highveld region and the diamond-rich East Griqualand area were most adversely affected.

In the middle of all of these momentous events the young leader Khama, chief of the Bamangwato and principal hero of the book, emerges. Like Moshoeshoe, he binds together disparate and displaced tribes, under the Bamangwato at his capital Shoshong, in northern Bechuanaland. While his father, Sekgoma, is still alive Khama controversially converts to Christianity and begins steering the tribe toward a rapprochement between traditional Tswana custom and Western practices. Central to this process is the role of the missionaries, two of whom (John MacKenzie and James Hepburn) also have a decisive hand in assisting Khama steer a safe course for his people in the turbulent currents of the time. Khama defers to these missionaries in all of his dealings with England, and their humanitarian outlook ensures that the Bamangwato under Khama remain relatively untouched by the dramatic events unfolding around them.

It is to Shoshong that Sebina leads his clan after coming under renewed threat from the resurgent Matabele under Lobengula. Like many other clans, they migrate to the safe haven that Khama has created in northern Bechuanaland. There they encounter the changes that Christianity has brought to traditional African customs and also become bemused observers of the watershed events of the last two decades of the nineteenth century. For another key figure has by this time staked a claim in the southern African hinterland: Cecil John Rhodes, in 1884 deputy commissioner for southern Bechuanaland.

The mineral discoveries of the time unlocked the avarice of the British colonial authorities, and Bechuanaland became seen as a crucial gateway to the north, to the legendary mineral-rich lands of Mashonaland and Matabeleland. Another key consideration was the quickening pace of Europe's scramble for Africa. At this time Germany claimed South West Africa, an act that alarmed the British authorities, who saw the danger of the Boer Republics linking up with this territory to the west. Again, Bechuanaland was the key to a regional settlement favorable to Britain: if the region could be placed under the British sphere of influence it could both provide a gateway to the north and also prize apart the potential allies Germany and the Boer Republics.

So Bechuanaland became "a bewitched crossroad," a territory in the eye of the storm sweeping southern Africa. After protracted negotiations, it was declared a British protectorate in 1885. It had to survive another stormy decade, however. Rhodes's grand plans for Mashonaland and Matabeleland were put into effect: Mashonaland was seized, and shortly afterward Lobengula was tricked into ceding his territory to Rhodes's conglomerate, the British South Africa Company. That the protectorate itself would also fall victim to the cynical machinations of Rhodes and his allies in the colonial administration seemed inevitable, until Rhodes overreached himself. The much-vaunted riches of Mashonaland and Matabeleland had come to nothing, and Rhodes turned his attention to the proven mineral riches of the Witwatersrand. In 1895 Leander Starr Jameson, friend and ally of Rhodes, launched his ill-fated invasion of the Transvaal Republic with the tacit support of the British government. He was ignominiously defeated after the planned uprising of the British Uitlanders in the Transvaal failed to materialize, and Rhodes was forced to resign as premier of the Cape Colony.

Crucially for Bechuanaland, the planned transfer of the protectorate to the British South Africa Company was postponed as a result of the Jameson Raid, and the matter never arose again. The protectorate was henceforth to exist as an independent entity and in 1966 became the fully independent state of Botswana. This is the triumphal conclusion to *A Bewitched Crossroad,* and Sebina, who survived the many storms that broke over the region at the time, is able at the story's end to slip peacefully into oblivion, assured that his clan is safe under the wise, benign leadership of Khama the Great.

This brief synopsis does not do justice to the immense complexity of the epic events Head describes in the text. Her broad canvas contains over 150 years of momentous history, from pre-Mfecane times to the declaration of the independent state of Botswana in 1966. It is this very complexity, however, that undoes the text in many ways. The early parts in particular contain a wealth of detail not strictly relevant to the main story line, and this serves merely to confound the reader. A contemporaneous review of the book summed up this weakness very aptly:

> A special effort is needed to perceive the different social and religious organisation of these people, and the names are tongue-twisting mind-benders. It is disheartening when you have painstakingly re-read several pages, sorted out the names of tribes and chiefs in your mind, only to have them perish forever on the very next page.
>
> The scene-setting is heavy going, and when the tribal story finally unfolds it is the familiar tale of colonialism all over again. I can only say

that I welcomed *A Bewitched Crossroad* onto my desk with expectations of
new discovery and insight, but closed it with a sense of baffled frustration.[2]

The central flaw of the text is its narrative structure. Sebina is clearly
intended to provide what Cherry Clayton, in one of the few full-length
articles on the book, calls "the focalising thread drawn through the historical tapestry."[3] As a firsthand witness to many of the most important
events of the period, he is able, it would seem, to provide a credible and
absorbing account of events while retaining a degree of detachment not
available to key figures like Khama or Rhodes. His view is quickly lost
in the maelstrom of events, however, and he reappears only sporadically
at various points in a narrative thread that is subordinate to the impersonal narrative view the omniscient narrator offers. *A Bewitched Crossroad*
is thus uncomfortably poised between impersonal historical narrative
and history as witnessed by a single participant.

Head was clearly influenced in her writing of this work by a seminal
precursor: Sol Plaatje's *Mhudi: An Epic of South African Native Life a Hun-
dred Years Ago* (1930). She was familiar with Plaatje's work; indeed, she
had written a foreword to the 1982 edition of his *Native Life in South
Africa* and was an ardent admirer. In his novel Plaatje also uses a broad
historical canvas and the focalizing thread of a hero and heroine who
participate in the events of the time. And although the novel has distinct weaknesses of its own—it is stylistically inelegant, ponderous, and
quaintly dated in places—Plaatje is more successful than Head in
achieving a balance between a sweeping historical narrative and a narrative that closely follows the perspectives of its hero and heroine.

That *A Bewitched Crossroad* is flawed says nothing about the value of
the book as a welcome reappraisal of the history of the southern African
region. By anchoring the story in the recollections of a single African
person and deploying a very sympathetic authorial narrator, Head provides an Afrocentric study, of a corrective sort, of the development of the
southern African region. The familiar contours of southern African history are given a fresh slant through the eyes and mind of the gently
musing Sebina.

Again, however, Head does not take full advantage of the occasions
for irony that this fresh perspective makes available. The grand historical narrative is allowed to dominate too much, and one does not
encounter familiar incidents rendered with the startling freshness and
clarity that is *Mhudi*'s great strength. In one of the most memorable of

such instances in Plaatje's novel, a group of young girls drawing water
are startled by a man who suddenly appears running in their direction:

> "Women, women," the fugitive, now almost in their midst, shouted at
> the top of his voice, panting heavily like a racehorse, "women, take to
> your legs and let them save you; never mind the water pots, save your
> lives. I have seen a milk-white house filled with a load of blood-red dev-
> ils, some hairy in the face, some smooth, some big, some small—devils in
> a moving white house crawling in this direction with all the sheep and
> cattle and livestock from Hades. Some of the devils had four legs, long
> tails and two heads—one head hairy and almost like that of a man, and
> the other shaped like that of a cow, but with great ears instead of horns.
> Women, run I say! The monsters are almost here."[4]

Only gradually does it dawn on the reader that he or she is seeing
recounted through the consciousness of an African the supposedly single
most important event of the period—the Voortrekkers' "Great Trek."
This time, however, the event is shrunk to less grandiose proportions
than it is given in conventional accounts by the implicit comparison
the novel makes between it and the far more calamitous events of the
Mfecane—events that have had a far more severe effect on the lives of
the people watching the arrival of the trekkers. Instead of being at the
center of the narrative, then, the trekkers arrive in medias res. Such profound and subtle irony is one of *Mhudi*'s major strengths.

Cherry Clayton claims greater success for *A Bewitched Crossroad* than I
have allowed here, arguing that it is Head's "fullest statement of her critique of South African history and society" (Clayton, 55). "By embed-
ding her act of protest within a celebration of a freer, more benevolent
culture and society," she goes on, "Head wins for herself and her project
a degree of freedom from the constriction within the protest paradigm
which has been the dominant mode for the black South African writer, a
mode in itself determined by the structures of apartheid" (56).

In her otherwise positive appraisal of the book Gillian Eilersen does
worry about its generic indeterminacy: "*A Bewitched Crossroad* can hardly
be called a historical novel in the sense that historical novels often have a
romantic, adventurous element, for its sticks too doggedly to historically verified events, though its angle is new. Nevertheless, the book is
formed as a novel: it has no list of contents, no maps, no index, though
all three would have been most useful" (Eilersen, 265). She neglects to
add (perhaps because it would upset her argument that the work is, on
balance, to be thought of as a novel) that it does have a list of references

at the end from which the quotations used liberally in the text are directly drawn. This, surely, is a highly unusual feature of a novel.

The point is that there is a great deal of disingenuity in the way Head constructs *A Bewitched Crossroad*. Her use of the Sebina figure is a dramatic device that lends credence to her rereading of southern African historiography while avoiding rigorous historical analysis. For Sebina's perceptions are in the end nothing other than those of the author, colored by what she takes to be the contemporary flavor of life at the time. And while she partly acknowledges this in an author's note at the outset, the work fails as a piece of fiction and yet cannot claim its place as a thoroughgoing historical work either.

Nonetheless, the painstaking research required for the book and Head's dedication to Botswana are irrefutable. The book was clearly her most ambitious project: in 1981 she had already published extracts from it prefaced by a description of the work as "my major obsession, the Khama novel."[5] And while it lacks the symmetry and clarity of focus that characterizes her other two works of this period, it is somewhat appropriate that this highly partisan work concludes the oeuvre of a writer whose own life was subject to the disruptive crosscurrents of southern African history but who came, in her own words, "by chance . . . to live in this village," which stands at the precise intersection of "a bewitched crossroad" (*Serowe,* x).

Chapter Eleven

Posthumously Published Works: *Tales of Tenderness and Power* (1989) and *A Woman Alone* (1990)

Two posthumous volumes of Head's uncollected writings have appeared. *Tales of Tenderness and Power* (1989) is a collection of short writings, some published, others previously unpublished but which, editor Gillian Eilersen notes, Head was in the process of assembling into a volume. A useful introduction precedes this miscellany of short pieces, giving a brief outline of Head's short and unhappy life. The pieces themselves defy neat categorization: some closely approximate the received notion of "fiction"; others are manifestly autobiographical. All of them, Eilersen claims, are closely rooted in actual events. This is not surprising, since Head's imagination was sparked by incidents she encountered in Botswanan village life and by stories other villagers told her.

The Serowe village milieu provides the backdrop for some of the pieces in *Tales of Tenderness,* although others originate from South Africa of the 1950s and 1960s. Two stories stand out, because of both their intrinsic merit and their South African setting: "The Prisoner Who Wore Glasses," which first appeared in 1973 and was subsequently reprinted in a dozen later anthologies, and "The Coming of the Christ-Child" (1981).

"The Prisoner Who Wore Glasses" is a tale about resilience, compassion, humanity, and brotherly feeling. A group of long-term political prisoners headed by their thin, myopic leader, called, appropriately, "Brille" ("Glasses"), comes into conflict with their new Afrikaans warder, Hannetjie. The group, called Span One, are no ordinary prisoners: "As political prisoners they were unlike the other prisoners in the sense that they felt no guilt nor were they outcasts of society. All guilty men instinctively cower, which was why it was the kind of prison where men got knocked out cold with a blow at the back of the head from an iron bar. Up until the arrival of Warder Hannetjie, no warder had dared beat any member of Span One and no warder had lasted more than a week with them. The battle was entirely psychological."[1]

Hannetjie is determined to subdue Span One. He catches Brille stealing grapes from the farm shed and has him confined to isolation for a week. He also discovers how Span One manage to conceal and eat half of the cabbages they are required to dig up on the prison farm, and they are punished. Then there is a dramatic turn of fortune: Warder Hannetjie is discovered by Brille in the act of stealing fertilizer and bribes him to keep quiet. Brille decides nonetheless to expose Hannetjie, and the warder is fined heavily. The psychological war continues until Hannetjie breaks down and pleads: "Brille . . . [t]his thing between you and me must end. You may not know it but I have a wife and children and you're driving me to suicide" ("Prisoner," 129–30). They enter into a pact: the prisoners are treated more humanely, and in return they steal certain commodities that Hannetjie needs for his farm. The message that Brille conveys to his children becomes the theme of the story: " 'Be good comrades, my children. Co-operate, then life will run smoothly' " (128).

"The Coming of the Christ-Child" is a tribute to Robert Sobukwe— leader of the Pan Africanist Congress when it broke away from the African National Congress in the 1950s. It is a fictionalized account of the passive resistance campaigns of the 1950s and 1960s, the rise of the ANC and the PAC, and their movement toward militancy. At the center of all this activity Head describes the life of a man who is born into a long line of mission-educated men whose family tradition is to become priests. The latest in this long tradition rejects this course: he is driven from a nonviolent stance to espouse increasingly militant ideas. He is ultimately detained in the general suppression of opposition movements in the 1960s, after becoming a highly vocal opponent of the National Party regime. He is sentenced to life imprisonment, then released after nine years but served with several banning orders.

The story ends on a premonitory note: nonviolent opposition to the state is no longer possible, and the freedom struggle is now going to be conducted along military lines:

> The crack-down on all political opposition was so severe that hundreds quailed and fled before the monstrous machine. It was the end of the long legend of non-violent protest. But a miracle people had not expected was that from 1957 onwards the white man was being system-

atically expelled from Africa, as a political force, as a governing power. Only the southern lands lay in bondage. Since people had been silenced on such a massive scale, the course and direction of events was no longer theirs. It had slipped from their grasp some time ago into the hands of the men who were training for revolution.[2]

The concluding sentence of the story is more characteristic of Head. It illustrates her sense that the writer's role "is to make life magical and to communicate a sense of wonder" (*Woman Alone*, 67): "When all was said and done and revolutions had been fought and won perhaps only dreamers longed for a voice like that of the man who was as beautiful as the coming of the Christ-Child" ("Christ-Child," 140).

These two stories provide a rare insight into the kind of writer Bessie Head might have been had she remained as preoccupied with South African themes and issues as were most of her contemporaries. Significantly, however, many of the other pieces in *Tales of Tenderness* caution against the corrupting influence of political power, a feature that is far more characteristic of her work, and others evoke for the reader the by now familiar texture of village life in Botswana. All bear the distinctive mark of their idiosyncratic author: they contain a rare power and freshness and, in the end, an elusive significance.

Many of the pieces included in *A Woman Alone* have been quoted extensively and commented on elsewhere in this study; the purpose of this section, then, is to provide an overview of the collection as a whole.

Like *Tales of Tenderness*, *A Woman Alone: Autobiographical Writings* (1990) collects pieces Head wrote in both South Africa and Botswana. The pieces are arranged roughly chronologically—from 1962 to 1985 (the years during which they were written)—and are divided into three periods, each of which is introduced by an autobiographical passage in which the author sets the scene for the period that follows. These introductory passages provide a narrative thread that links the three major periods of her life: her early life in South Africa (1937–1964), her period of exile in Botswana (1964–1979) and finally her life as a Botswanan citizen (1979–1986).

The focus of *A Woman Alone* is not principally on the writer Bessie Head's oeuvre but on the life of a South African–born woman who happened to become an internationally recognized author. The writings that make up this collection, in other words, present a piecemeal portrait of this life, a mosaic of sketches, essays, and personal notes, making the work a primarily biographical study.

There is a small but significant overlap between the two posthumous collections that attests interestingly to Head's defiance of the boundaries that traditionally exist between literary genres. The generic classification of the pieces in *A Woman Alone* poses a special challenge to the literary critic. The pieces span a number of overlapping genres: letters, journalism, autobiography, fictional sketches, essays, forewords, explanatory notes on novels. These generic markers do not denote discrete and insular categories, however. "Snowball: A Story," for example, should on the strength of its title be classified as a fictional sketch, but three-quarters of the piece is devoted to the author's reflections on her day-to-day life in District Six. Another example is "An African Story": its title promises fictional narrative, and indeed it begins like a story but then quickly becomes autobiographical, even anecdotal, and ends with a philosophical reflection on the future of South Africa. This indeterminacy characterizes almost every piece in the volume.

The majority of the pieces assembled in *A Woman Alone* defy classification. At their two extremes they represent autobiography and (very nearly) pure fiction. Most of them are, however, strung somewhere between these two extremes, and (with a few exceptions) each represents an amalgam of self-reflection, semifictional narrative, journalistic reportage, and cultural comment. The significance of each piece is that it reveals something about the extraordinary life of the author Bessie Head.

Chapter Twelve
The Critics' View

Bessie Head's works attracted critical attention from the early 1970s, with the appearance of her first three novels, but it took a few more years for the spate of early reviews to give way to more considered, full-length articles. What follows is a brief overview of some of the more substantial articles to have emerged in the last 20 years.

The first landmark article was Arthur Ravenscroft's influential "The Novels of Bessie Head" (1976), which set the tone for much of what was to follow. Ravenscroft argued that with novels by such writers as Peter Abrahams, Nadine Gordimer, Es'kia Mphahlele, and Bessie Head "we can begin to talk of a new category of South African novel, which, in theme at least, may be termed the South African Novel of Africa, concerned certainly with the viciousnesses of South Africa's political kingdom, but seeing them in meaningful relation to South Africa's future, by means of present models for that future at hand for close observation in the independent countries of Africa" (Ravenscroft, 174). He does not take this argument much further, however, noting only that Head's novels "strike a special chord for the South African diaspora" (174).

Describing the novels as "strange, ambiguous, deeply personal books which initially do not seem to be 'political' in any ordinary sense of the word," Ravenscroft goes on to refer to their "seeming emphasis on the quest for personal contentment, the abdication of political kingship—metaphorically in *When Rain Clouds Gather,* literally in *Maru,* and one might say wholesale in *A Question of Power*" (Ravenscroft, 175). This in itself, as critics over the years were often to observe, sets Head's work apart from that of her more overtly political South African contemporaries. Ravenscroft's other influential observation was to note the close relatedness of Head's novels: "It is precisely this journeying into the various characters' most secret interior recesses of mind and . . . of soul, that gives the three novels a quite remarkable cohesion and makes them a sort of trilogy." Each novel, he observes, "both strikes out anew, and also re-shoulders the same burden" (175).

Ravenscroft's appraisal of the novels is largely positive: he concludes by describing Head's creative imagination as having a "disturbing toughness" and praises her for refusing to offer "anything as facile as universal brotherhood and love for a political blueprint for either South Africa or all of Africa" (Ravenscroft, 186, 185). He does point out some weaknesses, however: "The precise relationship between individual freedom and political independence, and between a guarded core of privacy and an unbudding towards others, may seem rather elusive, perhaps even mystical, in my reading of the novel, and I see it as one of the weaknesses of *When Rain Clouds Gather*" (178–79). He also alludes to the "moments of melodrama and excessive romanticism" in *Rain Clouds* and declares himself uncertain whether, in *Maru,* "interior experience" and politics are "satisfyingly fused" (Ravenscroft, 179, 183).

In his 1979 article, Kolawole Ogungbesan traces the dynamic of "alienation and commitment" in Head's works. Arguing that Head "fits into a pattern which is now familiar to the whole world—the writer in exile," he goes on to observe that her "fierce determination to take root and grow in this unfamiliar terrain accounts for her distinctive vision of alienation."[1] Echoing Ravenscroft's observation that Head's apoliticism may irritate her more militant contemporaries, Ogungbesan notes that "while she, like other South African exiles, rejects the religious, social and intellectual order of her home country, she also rejects as completely the political visions which other African writers have posited as alternatives" (Ogungbesan, 206). What makes Head distinctive among African writers, he argues, is the sense she gives of "a much wider commitment to the main ethical and social attitudes of the world at large" and that she makes "alienation not an endless discovery demanding expression, but merely the initial premise" (207). In her novels Head explores the "possibilities of love . . . [as] the most potent antidote to alienation" and is, Ogungbesan concludes, "more willingly than most of her fellow exiles . . . content to settle down organically in her new environment" (209, 212).

Ogungbesan's understanding that Head was willing and able to take root in her new environment is based entirely on her public pronouncements on the issue, especially her lyrical eulogies, such as "For Serowe: A Village in Africa" (1965). Her private ruminations on the matter, as we saw in earlier chapters, were until the end of her life of an altogether more ambiguous nature.

Jean Marquard came much closer to her subject when she interviewed Head for an article that appeared in *London Magazine* (1979–1980). The article intersperses commentary with verbatim extracts from the interview and reveals much about the genesis and distinctive texture of

Head's writings. It also contains much fascinating commentary by Head on her own works and her circumstances in Botswana: "I have liked Botswana very much although I have got nothing out of loving a country that didn't want me" (Marquard, 51–52). Talking about her struggle to survive and her isolation, she remarks: "I have much in common with Olive Schreiner—I too have a pioneering role as she did. I have been concerned myself with the trends that will evolve in Southern Africa, with independence. I'm caught between the times Africa was not independent and when it was" (52–53). She also acknowledges a tendency to "an intense moral view" and "moral preachiness" in her earlier novels, whereas with *A Question of Power* "the question is left so open" (53). Marquard's interview set a trend: in the years that followed, Head was interviewed dozens of times, over 20 of which were either broadcast or published. Marquard concludes her article by noting a thematic development in Head's first three novels that "reveals a consistent movement inwards from a social to a metaphysical treatment of human insecurities and in the last novel the problem of adaptation to a new world, or new schemes of values, is located in the mind of a single character" (60). Head's achievement, finally, is to have fused "the ideal of community and brotherhood with a belief in the value of the one over the many" (61).

Cherry Wilhelm's article, "Bessie Head: The Face of Africa" (1983), continues this idea of the close relatedness and the increasingly inward movement of Head's novels: "The three novels . . . share a basic quest pattern, which moves in a suggestive direction. The protagonist struggles to find a self and a home, to 'belong' in both the geographical and existential sense" (Wilhelm, 2). She detects in the novels a "growing stress" on the "psychic arena" and argues for a sequential movement away from the realism of *Rain Clouds,* through the allegorical mode of *Maru,* to the almost entirely inner, psychic struggle of Elizabeth in *A Question of Power.* Head, she argues, becomes progressively more concerned with the "symbolic and metaphysical significance" of personal events (2). She praises *A Question of Power* particularly for its "striking . . . correlation of inner and outer worlds" and concludes that the novel's final affirmation is "not merely of individual integrity regained, nor of individual integration into a new community. It celebrates the release of the woman and the artist" (11, 12).

From articles that considered Head's first three novels in relation to each other, the focus gradually intensified. Individual works became the exclusive focus of attention, especially in the case of *A Question of Power,*

to which some 20 were devoted in the 1980s. The theme of woman
writers and the fictional treatment of madness is the broad, unifying element and is taken to almost clinical extremes in such articles as
Adetokunbo Pearse's "Apartheid and Madness: Bessie Head's *A Question
of Power*" (1983) and Elizabeth Evasdaughter's "Bessie Head's *A Question
of Power* Read as a Mariner's Guide to Paranoia" (1989).[2] Pearse begins
by arguing that "no work in the corpus of African literature dealing
with the theme of madness . . . captures the complexity and intensity of
the insane mind as does Bessie Head's *A Question of Power*" and goes on
to claim that "Bessie Head seems governed by the Freudian assertion
that the sexual libido is central to man's psychic behaviour" (Pearse, 81,
82). Evasdaughter takes the process of psychoanalytic reading a step
further by arguing that "while an author cannot be diagnosed from a literary text, a character can be" and that "Elizabeth, the center of consciousness in *A Question of Power*, meets the criteria . . . for paranoid
schizophrenia" (Evasdaughter, 71).

Despite the book's poor performance in the marketplace, critics generally agree that *A Question of Power* should be considered Head's major
work. In his review of the novel Charles Larson argued that with it Head
"has almost single-handedly brought about the inward turning of the
African novel."[3] In a subsequent article he expanded on this notion:
"Novels by African women are still a fairly rare occurrence. Introspective novels by African writers tend to be equally rare in large part
because the situational novel tends to be concerned with external events
instead of internal states of mind. Bessie Head's *A Question of Power* is
important not solely because it is an introspective novel by an African
woman but because the topics of her concern are also, for the most part,
foreign to African fiction . . . madness, sexuality, guilt."[4] As a final acco-
lade, the journal the *Black Scholar* ranked *A Question of Power* eighth in its
list of the 15 most influential books of the decade.[5]

As this overview of criticism suggests, Bessie Head's novels have been
overwhelmingly well received by critics over the years. Although doubts
about the integration of the private and public spheres in the construction of the first two novels have been repeatedly articulated, *When Rain
Clouds Gather* and *Maru* were generally received as promising early novels by an emerging writer. *Maru* particularly has continued to stimulate
discussion and debate, although the inherent problems of the text have
increasingly come to the fore. Margaret Daymond's article "Bessie
Head, *Maru,* and a Problem in Her Visionary Fable" (1989) is perhaps
the most sustained critique in this regard.[6]

The last three works that Head saw published in her lifetime have
attracted less attention than her early novels. Among them, only *The
Collector of Treasures* has received its full share of attention. In his review,
Michael Thorpe pointed out that the collection's subtitle, *and Other
Botswana Village Tales,* "indicates her kinship with the village storyteller
of the oral tradition" and suggested that the stories "lend themselves
especially well to an understanding of Head's aims as a writer."[7] She
wishes, like other African writers such as Ngugi and Achebe, "to present, in a human and humane light, African life before as well as after
the white man's coming" but seems "more troubled than they by the
contradictions within customary life" (Thorpe, 414). Her stories therefore often seem to be told "as an exploration, as a way to develop or even
question her own understanding" (414). "In Bessie Head's telling," he
concludes, "there is pain enough, but it is pain relieved constantly by
the clear light of a compassionate, understanding heart" (416).

Sara Chetin's lengthy article on *The Collector of Treasures* focuses on the
role that "myth plays in shaping human consciousness" in the stories as
well as on how Head's "concept of exile has influenced the way she perceives the art of oral storytelling" and how she explores "the neglected
realm of female experience."[8] Because Head grew up with "no particular
sense of belonging to a particular tribe or ethnic group," she had an " 'outsider' status" that she "consciously exploits . . . in her art by deliberately
distancing herself from the community whose tales she narrates so that
her stories reveal a distinctly ambiguous, unresolved tone" (Chetin, 114).

Serowe: Village of the Rain Wind has been respectfully received, although
as Gillian Eilersen noted, "[T]he fact that it appeared only in England,
in a paperback edition, meant that it attracted much less critical attention than *A Question of Power* had done" (Eilersen, 246–47). Its unusual-
ness in generic terms has also meant that it has not received the attention it deserves. Cherry Clayton's 1983 article " 'A World Elsewhere':
Bessie Head as Historian," which considers both *Serowe* and *A Bewitched
Crossroad,* is one of the few full-length treatments of the last two works
Head saw published in her lifetime.

Extracts from Clayton's article have been quoted in a previous chapter, but she raises some further points that are appropriate to mention
here. She argues that Head's "project as a writer, both as novelist and
historian . . . has been complex, relying on an interweaving of Western
literacy and the African oral tradition, thus creating, in its artistic
matrix, an imaginative equivalent of her moral and social ideal for
Southern Africa" (Clayton, 55). Clayton also argues for the close interre-

latedness of Head's last two works and sees *Serowe* as the "germ" of the later work: "Many of the elements and procedures of her 'African saga' were present in *Serowe* in a different proportion and emphasis; they lie loosely in a less deeply fused structure" (57–58). Clayton concludes: "Her unique position as a black woman historian in Southern Africa leads her to overturn a dominant settler mythology and to correct the harshness of the frontier spirit in favour of what she calls, in *The Collector of Treasures,* a 'compromise of tenderness' between African tradition and Western influence" (65).

Before her death in April 1986, Bessie Head had already achieved a respected place in the African literary world. Like countless writers before her, however, it took the shock of her premature death and the rounding off of her oeuvre for the literary world to place in perspective her stature and her inspirational role for other (mainly black woman) writers. An index of the gathering pace of Head scholarship from the mid-1980s onward is that the first edition of *Bessie Head: A Bibliography* (1986) listed fewer than 200 items by or about the writer; six years later, the second edition of the bibliography listed nearly 700 items, over half of which appeared after 1986.

Three book-length works on Head's writing have also recently appeared. The first is Virginia Ola's *Life and Works of Bessie Head* (1994),[9] which examines Head's works in terms of various themes: the question of good and evil, the role of women and nature in Head's works, and Head's role as storyteller and historian. Huma Ibrahim's *Bessie Head: Subversive Identities in Exile* (1996), a longer and more substantial work, looks at all of Head's works through the lens of Head's interest in the notion of identity—both individual and collective. Ibrahim's reading of Head offers highly theorized ways of entering into the discourse of her works: "What I am trying to bring to a reading of Head is an inclusion of her problematic examinations of nations, individuals, societies, history, exile, gender, and women's subversive identities as they become part of a larger sociopolitical framework of issues relating to Third World feminisms and postcoloniality."[10] A similar preoccupation with identity characterizes Maria Olaussen's *Forceful Creation in Harsh Terrain: Place and Identity in Three Novels by Bessie Head* (1997). The polarities of identity and the issues of female identity and women's experience are probed in six chapters that deal in turn with *When Rain Clouds Gather, Maru,* and *A Question of Power.*[11]

Head's achievements are largely the result of an uncompromising attitude toward her work and toward her life in general. When most of her South African contemporaries went into exile in Britain, Europe, and the United States—Dennis Brutus, Lewis Nkosi, Es'kia Mphahlele, and Bloke Modisane, among many others—Head chose neighboring Botswana, by South African standards then a dry, dusty, and undeveloped backwater. And whereas her fellow writers chose the depredations of apartheid South Africa as the subject matter for their searing social indictments, Head turned for inspiration to local sources and recorded in stories of parablelike intensity the daily lives of people in a remote African village. Despite a marked unevenness in the works constituting her oeuvre, her writing evinces an uncompromising conviction and personal integrity that demand that it be taken seriously.

Conclusion

As much of the foregoing discussion has suggested, it is useful to think of the work of Bessie Head as falling into two phases: an "inwardly directed" phase consisting of her first three published novels, *When Rain Clouds Gather* (1968), *Maru* (1971), and *A Question of Power* (1973), followed by a period of more "outwardly directed" or "socially oriented" work—*The Collector of Treasures* (1977), *Serowe: Village of the Rain Wind* (1981), and *A Bewitched Crossroad* (1984).

Some illuminating remarks about her work are conveyed in an article Head published in 1984:

> I hope two disparate worlds could be considered to have combined harmoniously in me. I have never been able in my writing to represent South African society but the situation of black people in South Africa, their anguish and their struggles, made its deep impress on me. From an earlier background, I know of a deep commitment to people, an involvement in questions of poverty and exploitation and a commitment to illuminating the future for younger generations. I needed an eternal and continuous world against which to work out these pre-occupations. (*Woman Alone*, 86)

The physical journey she undertook from South Africa to Botswana has a special resonance in her works. She journeys from disintegration to wholeness, from alienation to commitment in both her life and her work. If South Africa provides the impetus for her work, Botswana provides the locale: "South Africa, with its sense of ravages and horror, has lost that image of an Africa, ancient and existing since time immemorial, but in Botswana the presence of the timeless and immemorial is everywhere—in people, in animals, in everyday life and in custom and tradition" (*Woman Alone*, 86).

Some years earlier, in a piece entitled "Some Notes on Novel Writing," Head had commented on her inability to communicate the black South African experience: "Twenty-seven years of my life was [*sic*] lived in South Africa but I have been unable to record this experience in any direct way, as a writer. . . . The environment completely defeated me, as a writer. I just want people to be people, so I had no way of welding all the people together into a cohesive whole" (*Woman Alone*, 61–62). As we saw, however, her early desire to be a writer and some of her first efforts are recorded in a series of articles she published mainly in the *New African* in the early 1960s. These early writerly manifestations to some extent contradict her statement just quoted.

Although she was not completely stifled as a writer in South Africa, Head clearly felt that Botswana provided an environment more conducive to her creative instincts and a setting in which to resolve the difficulties that had confronted her as a writer in South Africa: ˙

> I have attempted to solve my problem by at least writing in an environment where all the people are welded together by an ancient order. Life in Botswana cannot be compared in any way to life in South Africa because here people live very secure lives, in a kind of social order shaped from centuries past by the ancestors of the tribe. I have tended to derive a feeling of security from this, so I could not be considered as a South African writer in exile, but as one who has put down roots. (*Woman Alone*, 62)

Her perception of Botswana was strongly influenced by her sense of its timelessness and durability, and she renders it in a characteristically lyrical, romantic idiom. She was never entirely absorbed by rural Botswana, however, and the novels reflect this tension. She herself was aware of this: "Such peaceful rural scenes would be hastily snatched to form the backdrop to tortuous novels. Perceptive fans sensed the disparity, the disparity between the peaceful simplicity of village life and a personality more complex than village life could ever be" (*Woman Alone*, 87).

This disparity was clearly a function of the author's own restlessness in her tranquil environment. The disjunction between Head's inner state and her outside world reaches a critical stage in *A Question of Power*, which explores the mind of the protagonist (with whom the author closely identifies herself) at the point of breakdown. *A Question of Power* is also a turning point, however. Head was from then on able to explore more objectively her adoptive land, and her later works evince little of the dramatic tension between character and setting that simultaneously mars her novels while charging them with their distinctive power. *The Collector of Treasures* and *Serowe: Village of the Rain Wind* (and *A Bewitched Crossroad* to a lesser extent) have a symmetry and harmoniousness of form that testify to the author's new sense of allegiance to Botswana. The concluding passage of her elegiac piece "A Search for Historical Continuity and Roots" captures something of the mood that infuses these works:

I have found the tensions and balances of the rural parts of Botswana, of a fine order. Enough of the ancient way of African life has survived to enable the younger generations to maintain their balance with comfort and ease, while almost daily with independence, new innovations, new concepts of government and critical, complex situations invade the life of the country. It is in such a world that one puts down some roots in the African soil and one finds a sense of peace about the future. (*Woman Alone*, 88)

Inner peace was ultimately to elude Head, however. She was never able fully to integrate with Botswanan society. In a letter written to Charles Sarvan in June 1980 she remarked: "I have looked back on my life here with extreme agony. . . . My novels and I never came in from the cold."[1] In many ways she never resolved the problems she encountered upon arriving in Botswana as a refugee, and although she achieved recognition as Botswana's preeminent writer and was granted citizenship in 1979, her feelings of alienation and deracination remained intense and debilitating. A remark she made on her arrival in Botswana therefore seems apposite as a description of her inner state on her death in April 1986: "Wherever I go I shall leave a chunk of myself here because I think of myself as a woman of Southern Africa—not as a black woman but as an ordinary and wryly humble woman. There was this immense conflict, pressure, uncertainty and insecurity that I have lived with for so long. I have solved nothing. I am like everyone else—perplexed, bewildered and desperate" (*Woman Alone*, 31).

In the end, however, it is the writing that endures, and it was in this arena that Head experienced some measure of control over a life that was always captive to the turbulent history of her time and place. Despite some of her own pronouncements on the matter, it was in Botswana, in the quiet rhythm of its daily life, and most important, in its continuity with the past that Bessie Head was able to carve out a spiritual as well as a physical home and work out in creative terms political alternatives for a more hopeful African future. Her role and achievements as a writer of Africa are most tellingly rendered, finally, in her own words:

I have always reserved a special category for myself, as a writer—that of a pioneer blazing a new trail into the future. It would seem as though Africa rises at a point in history when world trends are more hopefully against exploitation, slavery and oppression—all of which has been synonymous with the name, Africa. I have recorded whatever hopeful trend was presented to me in an attempt to shape the future, which I hope will be one of dignity and compassion. (*Woman Alone*, 64)

Notes and References

Chapter One

1. Kenneth Stanley Birch, "The Birch Family: An Introduction to the White Antecedents of the Late Bessie Amelia Head," *English in Africa* 22, no. 1 (May 1995): 7; hereafter cited in text.

2. Gillian Stead Eilersen, *Bessie Head: Thunder behind Her Ears: Her Life and Writing* (Portsmouth, N.H.: Heinemann; London: James Currey; Cape Town: Philip, 1995), 4; hereafter cited in text.

3. Bessie Head, *A Woman Alone: Autobiographical Writings,* ed. Craig MacKenzie (Oxford: Heinemann, 1990), xx; hereafter cited in text as *Woman Alone.*

4. Eilersen notes that the official cause of death was given as both "lung abscess" and "mental disorder," the latter specified as "dementia praecox"—a now obsolete term, she says, "for schizophrenia and characterised by a premature and marked decline from a former level of intellectual capacity, manifesting itself in apathy, depression or personality disintegration" (Eilersen, 9).

5. Kenneth Birch remarks: "Who the father was is completely unknown, and speculation is a waste of time. The event must have taken place in Johannesburg when Toby was out on parole from the family home; a brief encounter; a misuse of her mental state? Was she waylaid? Was she enticed somewhere? We do not know" (Birch, 10). Eilersen comments as follows: "There is no record of how it happened or where. Perhaps it was in Johannesburg before she left for the coast; or shortly after her arrival in Durban. But it is interesting to note in this connection the date of the drawing up of her will: October 1936. It is possible that some dramatic turn of events in her life—a love affair or a rape—could have occasioned it" (Eilersen, 7).

6. Randolph Vigne, ed., *A Gesture of Belonging: Letters from Bessie Head, 1965–1979* (London: SA Writers; Portsmouth, N.H.: Heinemann, 1991), 58; hereafter cited in text.

7. Bessie Head, "Dear Tim, Will You Please Come to My Birthday Party . . .," in *One Parent Families,* ed. Dulan Barber (London: Davis-Poynter, 1975), 110.

8. Head did not change even the name of the character who features in the novel, and from all accounts her portrayal accurately describes the Margaret Cadmore she knew from her days in the home.

9. Bessie Head to Margaret Cadmore, 10 September 1958, St. Monica's Home, Wentworth, Durban, South Africa, 1; hereafter cited in text as Cadmore 1958a.

10.   Head to Cadmore, 26 September 1958, St. Monica's Home, Wentworth, Durban, South Africa, 2; hereafter cited in text as Cadmore 1958b.

11.   See Michelle Adler et al., "Bessie Head," in *Between the Lines: Interviews with Bessie Head, Sheila Roberts, Ellen Kuzwayo, Miriam Tlali*, ed. Craig MacKenzie and Cherry Clayton (Grahamstown, South Africa: National English Literary Museum, 1989), 5–30; hereafter cited in text as *Between the Lines*.

12.   James Matthews, "Scores with First Novel," *Cape Times Weekend Magazine* (26 July 1969): 9; hereafter cited in text.

13.   Eilersen argues that Head's first violent sexual encounter "casts much light on Bessie Emery's later attitude to sex" (Eilersen, 49).

14.   Bessie Head, "Things I Don't Like," *New African* 1, no. 7 (1962): 10.

15.   For details see Paulette Coetzee and Craig MacKenzie, "Bessie Head: Rediscovered Early Poems," *English in Africa* 23, no. 1 (1996): 29–39.

16.   Bessie Head, "Unpublished Early Poems," *English in Africa* 23, no. 1 (1996): 40–46.

17.   Head to unknown recipient, ca. 1962, accession no. 96.1, National English Literary Museum, Grahamstown, South Africa, 1.

18.   Bessie Head, "Dollar Brand," ca. 1960, accession no. 96.1, National English Literary Museum, Grahamstown, South Africa, 2.

19.   Bessie Head, "Untitled Now," *English in Africa* 23, no. 1 (1994): 44–45.

20.   Susan Gardner showed remarkable prescience in this regard, noting that Head's "early pastoral poetry" (here Gardner is picking up on Matthews's references, quoted earlier in the text) "could well prefigure the evocative descriptions of the early harsh Botswanan landscape." See Gardner, introduction to *Bessie Head: A Bibliography* (Grahamstown, South Africa: National English Literary Museum, 1986), 6.

21.   Bessie Head, "Untitled Now," 43.

22.   Brutus escaped from prison but was rearrested and incarcerated on Robben Island before leaving South Africa on an exit permit in 1966.

Chapter Two

1.   Bessie Head, *The Cardinals: With Meditations and Stories* (Cape Town: Philip, 1993), 23–24; hereafter cited in text as *Cardinals*.

2.   Margaret Daymond, introduction to Head, *The Cardinals*, xi–xii.

3.   Seven previously unpublished short pieces accompany the main story. The pieces that make up this small miscellany—aptly characterized by Daymond's subtitle "Meditations and Stories"—were penned shortly after Head arrived in Botswana and provide glimpses of her inner turmoil at this critical time. "Africa" and "Earth Love" stand out among them; the latter particularly reveals a wry humor and courage remarkable in someone fleeing a South African childhood of such unimaginable horror.

Chapter Three

1. Bessie Head to Dorothea Ewan, 30 September 1972, accession no. 92.2.1, National English Literary Museum, Grahamstown, South Africa, 1; hereafter cited in text as Head 1972.
2. Head to Ewan, 28 January 1973, accession no. 92.2.3, National English Literary Museum, Grahamstown, South Africa, 1.
3. Head to Ewan, 26 March 1973, accession no. 92.2.4, National English Literary Museum, Grahamstown, South Africa, 1; hereafter cited in text as Head 1973a.
4. Head to Ewan, 9 August 1973, accession no. 92.2.6, National English Literary Museum, Grahamstown, South Africa, 1; hereafter cited in text as Head 1973b.
5. Head to Ewan, 27 December 1973, accession no. 92.2.8, National English Literary Museum, Grahamstown, South Africa, 1; hereafter cited in text as Head 1973c.

Chapter Four

1. Head, *When Rain Clouds Gather* (London: Heinemann Educational, 1972), 16; hereafter cited in text as *Rain Clouds*.
2. Simon Simonse, "African Literature between Nostalgia and Utopia: African Novels Since 1953 in the Light of the Modes-of-Production Approach," *Research in African Literatures* 31, no. 4 (1982): 468.
3. Arthur Ravenscroft, "The Novels of Bessie Head," in *Aspects of South African Literature,* ed. Christopher Heywood (London: Heinemann, 1976), 178–79; hereafter cited in text.

Chapter Five

1. Bessie Head, *Maru* (London: Heinemann, 1972), 12; hereafter cited in text.
2. Cherry Wilhelm [Clayton], "Bessie Head: The Face of Africa," *English in Africa* 10, no. 1 (1983): 10; hereafter cited in text.
3. Susan Gardner suggested the link between *Maru* and the King Cophetua tale. See her introduction to *Bessie Head: A Bibliography* (Grahamstown, South Africa: National English Literary Museum, 1986), 7.

Chapter Six

1. Bessie Head, *A Question of Power* (London: Heinemann, 1974), 16; hereafter cited in text as *Power*.
2. Head, "Tao," in *Tales of Tenderness and Power* (Oxford: Heinemann, 1990), 48–55.
3. Head, "The Green Tree," in *Tales of Tenderness and Power,* 47.

4. John Berger, *Pig Earth* (London: Writers and Readers, 1979), 208; hereafter cited in text.

Chapter Seven

1. Linda Susan Beard, "Bessie Head, Cape Gooseberry, and the Question of Power," *ALA Bulletin* 12, no. 2 (1986): 41.

Chapter Eight

1. Bessie Head, *The Collector of Treasures and Other Botswana Village Tales* (London: Heinemann, 1977), 1; hereafter cited in text as *Collector*.
2. Walter J. Ong, *Orality and Literacy: The Technologizing of the Word* (London: Methuen, 1982), 140.
3. Bessie Head, "Arts and Africa," interview by Anne Bolsover about Head's writing, BBC World Service, 17 June 1981, transcript 392G: 1.
4. Walter Benjamin, "The Storyteller: Reflections on the Works of Nikolai Leskov," in *Illuminations* (London: Fontana/Collins, 1973), 87.

Chapter Nine

1. Bessie Head, *Serowe: Village of the Rain Wind* (London: Heinemann, 1981), xiv; hereafter cited in text as *Serowe*.
2. Lorna de Smidt, "Where Rain Is Paramount," *Africa Now* 7 (October 1981): 101; hereafter cited in text.

Chapter Ten

1. Bessie Head, *A Bewitched Crossroad: An African Saga* (Johannesburg: Ad. Donker, 1984).
2. Barry Ronge, review of *A Bewitched Crossroad, Fair Lady* (20 March 1985): 27.
3. Cherry Clayton, " 'A World Elsewhere': Bessie Head as Historian," *English in Africa* 15, no. 1 (1988): 59; hereafter cited in text.
4. Sol T. Plaatje, *Mhudi,* rev. ed. (London: Heinemann, 1978), 89–90.
5. Bessie Head, "A Bewitched Crossroad," *The Bloody Horse* 3 (1981): 5.

Chapter Eleven

1. Bessie Head, "The Prisoner Who Wore Glasses," in *Tales of Tenderness and Power* (Oxford: Heinemann, 1990), 126; hereafter cited in text as "Prisoner."
2. Head, "The Coming of the Christ-Child," in *Tales of Tenderness and Power,* 140; hereafter cited in text as "Christ-Child."

Chapter Twelve

1. Kolawole Ogungbesan, "The Cape Gooseberry Also Grows in Botswana: Alienation and Commitment in the Writings of Bessie Head," *Journal of African Studies* 6 (1979–1980): 206; hereafter cited in text.

2. Adetokunbo Pearse, "Apartheid and Madness: Bessie Head's *A Question of Power*," *Kunapipi* 5, no. 2 (1983): 81–93; Elizabeth Evasdaughter, "Bessie Head's *A Question of Power* Read as a Mariner's Guide to Paranoia," *Research in African Literatures* 20, no. 1 (1989): 72–83.

3. Charles R. Larson, "Anglophone Writing from Africa," *Books Abroad* 48, no. 3 (1974): 521.

4. Charles R. Larson, "The Singular Consciousness," in *The Novel in the Third World* (Washington, D.C.: Inscape, 1976), 165.

5. Margaret Walker Alexander, "Most Influential Books for the Decade," *Black Scholar* 12 (1981): 92.

6. Margaret Daymond, "Bessie Head, *Maru,* and a Problem in Her Visionary Fable," in *Short Fiction in the New Literatures in English,* ed. J. Bardolph (Nice, France: Faculté des Lettres et Sciences Humaines, 1989), 247–52.

7. Michael Thorpe, "Treasures of the Heart: The Short Stories of Bessie Head," *World Literature Today* 57, no. 3 (1983): 414; hereafter cited in text.

8. Sara Chetin, "Myth, Exile, and the Female Condition: Bessie Head's *The Collector of Treasures,*" *Journal of Commonwealth Literature* 24, no. 1 (1989): 114; hereafter cited in text.

9. Virginia Ola, *The Life and Works of Bessie Head* (Lewiston, Idaho: Edwin Mellen Press, 1994).

10. Huma Ibrahim, *Bessie Head: Subversive Identities in Exile* (Charlottesville: University Press of Virginia, 1996), 22.

11. Maria Olaussen, *Forceful Creation in Harsh Terrain: Place and Identity in Three Novels by Bessie Head* (Frankfurt am Main: Peter Lang, 1997).

Conclusion

1. Charles Sarvan, "Bessie Head: Two Letters," *Wasafiri* 12 (1990): 15.

Selected Bibliography

PRIMARY SOURCES

When Rain Clouds Gather. New York: Simon and Schuster, 1968; London: Gollancz, 1969.

Maru. London: Gollancz; New York: McCall, 1971.

A Question of Power. London: Davis Poynter; New York: Pantheon, 1973.

The Collector of Treasures and Other Botswana Village Tales. London: Heinemann; Cape Town: David Philip, 1977.

Serowe: Village of the Rain Wind. London: Heinemann; Cape Town: David Philip, 1981.

A Bewitched Crossroad: An African Saga. Johannesburg: Ad. Donker, 1984.

Tales of Tenderness and Power. Ed. Gillian Stead Eilersen. Johannesburg: Ad. Donker, 1989; Oxford: Heinemann, 1990.

A Woman Alone: Autobiographical Writings. Ed. Craig MacKenzie. Oxford: Heinemann, 1990.

A Gesture of Belonging: Letters from Bessie Head, 1965–1979. Ed. Randolph Vigne. London: SA Writers; Portsmouth, N.H.: Heinemann, 1991.

The Cardinals: With Meditations and Stories. Ed. M. J. Daymond. Cape Town: David Philip, 1993; Oxford: Heinemann, 1995.

SECONDARY SOURCES

Books

Abrahams, Cecil, ed. *The Tragic Life: Bessie Head and Literature in Southern Africa.* Trenton, N.J.: Africa World Press, 1990. A collection of 11 essays by various contributors that cover aspects of Head's life and works.

Eilersen, Gillian Stead. *Bessie Head: Thunder behind Her Ears: Her Life and Writing.* Portsmouth, N.H.: Heinemann; London: James Currey; Cape Town: David Philip, 1995. A comprehensive biography of Bessie Head that includes some discussion of her works.

Ibrahim, Huma. *Bessie Head: Subversive Identities in Exile.* Charlottesville: University Press of Virginia, 1996. Highly theorized examination of all of Head's works with particular attention to Head's concern with issues of identity. Head's six works of fiction are examined in separate chapters, which are concerned especially with the challenge Head's texts pose to conventional interpretations of postcoloniality and feminism in a Third World context.

MacKenzie, Craig. *Bessie Head: An Introduction*. Grahamstown, South Africa: National English Literary Museum, 1989. A brief introductory overview of Head's life and work.

MacKenzie, Craig, and Catherine Woeber. *Bessie Head: A Bibliography*. Grahamstown, South Africa: National English Literary Museum, 1992. A comprehensive bibliography of primary and secondary sources listing some 700 items.

Ola, Virginia Uzoma. *The Life and Works of Bessie Head*. Lewiston, Idaho: Edwin Mellen Press, 1994. A short examination of Head's writing that pays special attention to certain unifying themes in her works, including good and evil, women's roles, and the role of nature.

Olaussen, Maria. *Forceful Creation in Harsh Terrain: Place and Identity in Three Novels by Bessie Head*. Frankfurt am Main: Peter Lang, 1997. An analysis of *When Rain Clouds Gather, Maru,* and *A Question of Power* that explores issues of identity and belonging, particularly in relation to women's experiences.

Articles

Adler, Michelle, et al. "Bessie Head." In *Between the Lines: Interviews with Bessie Head, Sheila Roberts, Ellen Kuzwayo, Miriam Tlali*. Ed. Craig MacKenzie and Cherry Clayton. Grahamstown, South Africa: National English Literary Museum, 1989, 5–30. Long interview conducted in 1983 by students and academics from the University of the Witwatersrand on a variety of aspects of Head's work.

Beard, Linda Susan. "Bessie Head's *A Question of Power*: The Journey through Disintegration to Wholeness." *Colby Library Quarterly* 15, no. 4 (December 1979): 267–74. Offers a clear, incisive perspective on Head's most difficult novel. Isolates the major religious coordinates of the novel (Judaism, Christianity, Buddhism, Hinduism, and classical mythology) and attempts to resolve the novel's many intractable paradoxes and polarities.

Birch, Kenneth Stanley. "The Birch Family: An Introduction to the White Antecedents of the Late Bessie Amelia Head." *English in Africa* 22, no. 1 (May 1995): 1–18. Landmark article that placed on public record for the first time the background of the Birch family and its relations with its relative Bessie Head.

Chetin, Sara. "Myth, Exile, and the Female Condition: Bessie Head's *The Collector of Treasures*." *Journal of Commonwealth Literature* 24, no. 1 (1989): 114. Long article that looks systematically at each of the stories. Explores issues relating to Head's use of myth, her attention to feminist issues, and the role of exile in her outlook and orientation.

Clayton, Cherry. " 'A World Elsewhere': Bessie Head as Historian." *English in Africa* 15, no. 1 (May 1988): 55–70. Establishes the relationship between *Serowe: Village of the Rain Wind* and *A Bewitched Crossroad* and examines the contributions of both histories to the overturning of colonial myths about the African hinterland.

Daymond, Margaret. "Bessie Head, *Maru*, and a Problem in Her Visionary Fable." In *Short Fiction in the New Literatures in English*, ed. J. Bardolph. Nice, France: Faculté des Lettres et Sciences Humaines, 1989, 247–52. Probes the central problems in the construction of *Maru* while offering an appreciative and astute reading of the novel.

Johnson, Joyce. "Metaphor, Myth, and Meaning in Bessie Head's *A Question of Power*." *World Literature Written in English* 25 (Autumn 1985): 198–211. Examines the novel by carefully considering its structure and its central concerns and motifs. Offers a reading that attempts to render comprehensible the events of the novel and the key concepts that the author employs.

———. "Bessie Head and the Oral Tradition: The Structure of *Maru*." *Wasafiri* 3 (Autumn 1985): 5–8. Examines *Maru* in relation to African myths, legends, and folktales. A rich insight into the mythological and universal resonances of the novel.

MacKenzie, Craig. "Short Fiction in the Making: The Case of Bessie Head." *English in Africa* 16, no. 1 (May 1989): 17–28. Explores the contiguity between the stories of *The Collector of Treasures* and the milieu of informal gossip and tales that characterizes contemporary village life in Botswana.

———. "Allegiance and Alienation in the Novels of Bessie Head." In *Essays on African Writing: A Reevaluation*, ed. Abdulrazak Gurnah. Oxford: Heinemann Educational, 1993, 111–25. Examines the relationship between Head's first three novels and argues that *A Question of Power* succeeds in resisting the narrative closure evident in the first two novels.

Marquard, Jean. "Bessie Head: Exile and Community in Southern Africa." *London Magazine* 18, nos. 9 and 10 (December 1978–January 1979): 48–61. Considers Head's novels and (then) unpublished social history of Serowe, interspersed with extracts from an interview. Offers a vivid picture of the writer's early life in South Africa and her day-to-day life in Serowe. Provides a useful introduction to a writer poised midway in her career.

Nkosi, Lewis. "Southern Africa: Protest and Commitment." In Nkosi, *Tasks and Masks: Themes and Styles of African Literature*. Harlow, England: Longman, 1981, 76–106. Discusses Head's first three novels alongside writing by other southern African authors, notably Lessing and Mphahlele, in a chapter devoted to an examination of the dynamic of protest and commitment in southern African writing of the 1950s and 1960s. Offers an informed critic's assessment of the respective merits and demerits of Head's novels.

Ogungbesan, Kolawole. "The Cape Gooseberry Also Grows in Botswana: Alienation and Commitment in the Writings of Bessie Head." *Présence Africaine* 109 (1979): 92–106. (Reprinted in *Journal of African Studies* 6 [1979–1980]: 206–12.) Explores the dynamic of alienation and commitment in Head's novels and stories. Contrasts her with fellow South African exiles and argues that her apolitical outlook, her willingness to take root in a neighboring African state, and her commitment to ordinary people set her apart from her South African contemporaries.

Ravenscroft, Arthur. "The Novels of Bessie Head." In *Aspects of South African Literature,* ed. Christopher Heywood. London: Heinemann, 1976, 174–86. Seminal work that places Head's novels in a new category of the South African novel by virtue of their vision for a future South Africa based on the models of independent African states. Argues that the novels reflect an increasing interiority of perspective, that each novel returns to the central issues of personal contentment and political power, and that each tries to resolve these issues in a different way.

Taiwo, Oladele. "Bessie Head." In Taiwo, *Female Novelists of Modern Africa.* London: Macmillan, 1984, 185–214. Useful general introduction to Head's novels, short stories (*The Collector of Treasures*), and social history (*Serowe: Village of the Rain Wind*). Discusses each work separately and in order of publication.

Thorpe, Michael. "Treasures of the Heart: The Short Stories of Bessie Head." *World Literature Today* 57, no. 3 (1983): 414–16. Brief but insightful overview of the short stories in *The Collector of Treasures.* Pays particular attention to the stories' relation to the oral milieu of Serowe.

Wilhelm [Clayton], Cherry. "Bessie Head: The Face of Africa." *English in Africa* 10, no. 2 (May 1983): 1–13. Densely allusive reading of Head's novels that evokes the texture of Head's fictive world as well as its greater sociohistorical resonance. Argues that the novels share a basic quest pattern in which the protagonist struggles to attain a sense of belonging in both a geographical and an existential sense.

Index

The Author

Craig MacKenzie was born in Durban, South Africa, and educated at the University of Natal and Rhodes University. He has worked at the National English Literary Museum in Grahamstown and is presently senior lecturer in the Department of English at the Rand Afrikaans University in Johannesburg. MacKenzie has published articles on South African literature in *English in Africa, World Literature Written in English, Research in African Literatures, Current Writing,* and *Journal of Southern African Studies* and has contributed to such books as *International Literature in English, Essays on African Writing, Reference Guide to Short Fiction,* and the *Routledge Encyclopedia of Post-Colonial Literatures in English,* for which he also acted as regional coeditor (South Africa). His book publications include two volumes of interviews with South African woman writers (entitled *Between the Lines*), *Bessie Head: An Introduction, Bessie Head: A Bibliography,* and *Nadine Gordimer: A Bibliography.* He is the editor of *A Woman Alone,* a collection of Bessie Head's autobiographical writings. MacKenzie has been editor of *English in Africa* since 1994 and is currently working on an anthology of South African short stories and new editions of the works of Herman Charles Bosman.

The Editor

Bernth Lindfors is a professor of English and African literatures at the University of Texas at Austin. He has written and edited more than 30 books, including *Black African Literature in English* (1979, 1986, 1989, 1995), *Popular Literatures in Africa* (1991), *Comparative Approaches to African Literatures* (1994), *Long Drums and Canons: Teaching and Researching African Literatures* (1995), *Loaded Vehicles: Studies in African Literary Media* (1996), and (with Reinhard Sander) *Twentieth-Century Caribbean and Black African Writers* (1992, 1993, 1996). From 1970 to 1989 he was editor of *Research in African Literatures*.